LISTENING IN

Intercepting German Trench
Communications in World War I

Ernest H. Hinrichs, Sr.

LISTENING IN

Intercepting German Trench Communications in World War I

by

Ernest H. Hinrichs

edited by

Ernest H. Hinrichs, Jr.

foreword by

Henry F. Schorreck

 **White Mane Books**

This White Mane Books publication
was printed by
Beidel Printing House, Inc.
63 West Burd Street
Shippensburg, PA 17257 USA
(White Mane Books is a division of White Mane Publishing Company, Inc.)

Unless otherwise noted, photos are the property of the author.

In respect for the scholarship contained herein, the acid-free paper used in this book meets the guidelines for permanence and durability of the Committee on Production Guidelines for Book Longevity of the Council on Library Resources.

For a complete list of available publications
please write
White Mane Publishing Company, Inc.
P.O. Box 152
Shippensburg, PA 17257 USA

Library of Congress Cataloging-in-Publication Data

Hinrichs, Ernest H., 1891-
    Listening in : intercepting German trench communications in World
War I / by Ernest H. Hinrichs ; edited by Ernest H. Hinrichs, Jr. ;
foreword by Henry F. Schorreck.
        p.   cm.
    Includes bibliographical references (p.   ) and index.
    ISBN 0-942597-78-8 (alk. paper)
    1. Hinrichs, Ernest H., 1891– – –Diaries.   2. World War, 1914-1918–
–Military intelligence– –United States.   3. World War, 1914-1918–
–Personal narratives, American.   4. Soldiers– –United States–
–Diaries.   5. United States. Army– –Biography.   I. Hinrichs, Ernest
H., 1922–.   II. Title.
D639.S7H565   1995
940.4' 8673– –dc20   95-19515
                                                                        CIP

PRINTED IN THE UNITED STATES OF AMERICA

CONTENTS

FOREWORD

There are other personal accounts, recollections, memoirs, of the fighting and life at the front as the participants lived it during World War I. In that regard, Sergeant Ernest Hinrichs' diary is not unique. What is different about Sergeant Hinrichs is what he did during the war. Sergeant Hinrichs was part of a brand new American intelligence activity—communications intelligence. Communications intelligence may be defined as the obtaining of information from the interception and processing of enemy communications. Processing includes, decoding and/or deciphering, translation, and dissemination of the intelligence.

The United States entered World War I with almost no military intelligence establishment and absolutely no communications intelligence organization. In May 1917, Major Ralph Van Deman, over the objections of the Army Chief of Staff, General Hugh Scott, had persuaded Secretary of War Newton D. Baker to create a separate military intelligence division as part of the General Staff. In June, Van Deman hired Herbert O. Yardley to direct MI-8, the Code and Telegraph Section of Military Intelligence. This was the cryptanalytic unit destined to gain fame as the "American Black Chamber."

While Yardley was organizing MI-8 for home-front activities, Van Deman turned his attention to organizing the intelligence and communications intelligence staffs for General John J. Pershing and the American Expeditionary Forces. Military intelligence on Pershing's staff was designated G2. The subsection of G2 responsible for the cryptanalysis of enemy codes and ciphers (among other things), was designated A6. Thus the cryptanalytic unit of the military intelligence section of the AEF headquarters staff was known as G2A6. There was a corresponding unit, called the Radio Intelligence Section which performed similar duties at the headquarters of the U.S. First and Second Armies.

The Radio Intelligence Section at the Army level had a number of functions. They were to receive, decode/decipher, and translate, intercepted enemy messages. They provided what was called then a goniometric service, which meant the construction of enemy order of battle intelligence by identifying and locating enemy forces and positions by means of radio direction finding. Goniometry or D/F, as it was later termed, also served, at times, to alert Allied ground forces of impending German air attacks. G2A6 and the Radio Intelligence Section also processed enemy press messages and translated enemy documents that pertained to radio and/or codes and ciphers. And they were also responsible for the administration of the process of monitoring U.S. radio and telephone communications.

Neither G2A6 nor the Radio Intelligence Sections at the Army level performed the actual radio intercept and D/F work. This was conducted by the Radio Section of the Signal Corps. (The original name of this unit was the Radio Intelligence Section of the Signal Corps.) It was responsible for providing the men and the equipment to operate the field intercept stations, the gonio or D/F stations, and the "listening stations." The stations were identified this way because of the different functions each performed. The field stations intercepted the German radio stations; the gonio stations did the D/F work, locating German division, corps, and army radio stations. The field stations also performed some basic cryptanalytic work. The U.S. had five intercept and eight gonio stations in the AEF.

The "listening stations" had three distinct functions: to intercept and decode German ground telegraph (T.P.S.) messages; to intercept German trench telephone conversations; and to monitor U.S. telephone communications in the front lines. This was the work to which Private, later Sergeant, Ernest Hinrichs was assigned.

T.P.S. was an abbreviation which represented the French phrase, "Telegraphie per le soil," or ground telegraph. Ground telegraph was a rather unusual means of communicating. A regular telegraph key was attached to a battery and the wires were led a short distance away and attached to a rod buried in the earth. Using the earth as a conductor, messages could be sent over short distances where another operator could, with antenna wires from a similar rod in the earth, running back to his receiver, pick up the transmissions from the sender. This eliminated the need to use radio and avoided the risks of normal telegraph lines being broken by shell-fire. The range was very limited but that was accepted. This was an established means of German trench communications between company and battalion headquarters.

Assignment to a listening station was more dangerous than to either the field intercept or gonio stations. The T.P.S. had a very short range and was used only in the forward areas, i.e., the trenches at the front lines. The Allied intercept operators, such as Sergeant Hinrichs, crawled out into no-man's-land between the trenches to either lay their antenna wire along the ground, creating a large induction loop or to stick a rod into the ground and attach their antenna leads to the rod. Through induction they could then intercept both the German T.P.S. messages and telephone conversations.

There was very close liaison among and between the men of the Radio Section of the Signal Corps, the Radio Intelligence Sections, and G2A6. In addition, the listening stations transmitted important tactical intelligence immediately to the nearest commander of troops so that urgent information could be acted upon without delay.

For those of us interested in the history of U.S. communications intelligence, Sergeant Hinrichs' diary is quite significant. We are aware of interviews of cryptanalysts who served in the AEF, and intercept operators from the Radio Intelligence Service who served on the Mexican border from 1918–1920, but so far as is known, there are no interviews or memoirs of AEF listening station intercept operators. Further, although there is written documentation about G2A6 and the field intercept and gonio stations, there is almost nothing on the listening stations or the men who operated them. So the diary has an intrinsic value because of the uniqueness of its content.

Secondly, it provides a very good account of a participant in a major U.S. communications deception operation late in the war. Lt. Col. Frank Moorman, Chief of G2A6, alluded briefly in his *Final Report of the Radio Intelligence Section, General Staff, General Headquarters, American Expeditionary Forces, 1918–1920*, to a communications deception operation in connection with the second phase of the Argonne-Meuse operation. It is fairly clear that the operation Sergeant Hinrichs described and the one mentioned by Moorman are the same. Without Sergeant Hinrichs' more detailed description of what the intercept operators did to deceive the Germans we would only have Moorman's few bland sentences telling us that an operation took place.

There are a few interesting points which emerge from the diary. One is that it has been known that our intercept operators used French radio equipment for intercept work. What has not been generally known was that the listening stations were manned by both American and French operators. My impression from the diary was that the listening stations had both until August 20, 1918. After that, either they were manned by Americans, or Hinrichs did not mention the French operators anymore. I do not believe that our field intercept or gonio stations had integrated French operators.

Another point which I believe requires further research, prompted by the diary, are Hinrichs' references to telephone intercepts. In his *Final Report*, Moorman stated that such intercepts were useful early in the war, but that later they were neither important nor frequent. Based on Hinrichs' references and even on other research, it might be suggested that although the frequency may have declined, their value did not. Perhaps more were received and acted upon at the division level (listening stations existed down to and including the division level) than Moorman was aware.

As is the case with the interviews and memoirs of other World War I participants in the then new business of communications intelligence, the more information about these activities and the men who engaged in them surfaces, the more respect and admiration we have for them. A small diary, kept by an unknown man, about an unknown activity in the Great War, certainly illuminates more of the history of U.S. communications intelligence and the pioneers who made that history.

Henry F. Schorreck

PREFACE

Upon arrival in France every soldier became keenly aware of the censorship. That military necessity which subjected letters to the review of one's superiors and which compelled the limiting of correspondence with the folks at home to the most general topics, made a diary notebook of some kind most important as a means of self expression. Here one's inmost thoughts could be recorded without restraint, and a sensitive or timid soul could express its reaction to the abnormal environment without fear of censor. In my case, the peculiar secret nature of my service made all reference to my work taboo in my letters home, and the notebook became a constant companion.

These writings have been taken for the most part verbatim from my notebook. For the sake of coherence and to avoid the numerous breaks and the disjointed sequence of the diary form, many entries have been brought together, and, at times, incidents have been rearranged in order to clarify the text or to add human interest. Large sections of the original have been omitted.

I want to make the definite statement that the incidents described in these pages actually took place. There has been a strong temptation to draw upon the imagination. I have consistently refused to do so, with the result that the text remains historical. That is, it is a true picture of my reaction to the war. The very definite change in point of view with experience is not so noticeable in the first part as it is in the more active sections which follow.

Ernest H. Hinrichs
1925

The material my father prepared in the 1920's and 1930's has been basically unchanged in the editing of the text. There have been corrections in spelling and grammar, with minor changes in sentence structure. Nothing has been deleted from or added to the original text. Introductory material has been prepared for each chapter. The footnotes indicated by asterisk are my father's original ones. When I believe that they were added later, I have so indicated. The appendices and endnotes are the result of my own efforts.

A cogent discussion of what motivates veterans to write accounts of their wartime experiences can be found in The New York Times Book Review of July 31, 1988. The lead article, "In The Whirl And Muddle Of War" by Samuel Hynes is worth the attention of readers interested in this phenomenon.

Ernest H. Hinrichs, Jr.
September 1994

ACKNOWLEDGEMENTS

I am deeply grateful to my family and friends who have supported me in my desire to publish this book, which was written over sixty years ago by my father. My brother, Dr. John Hinrichs, shared with me the desire to preserve this material for historical record, but since I had retired from active practice, delegated the task to me. I am very grateful for his criticism and support. My good friend, John Howell, coached me on the vagaries of the computer and taught me word processing. My daughter, Dr. Gail Heyn, her husband, Pinhas, and their children, Ben, Aviva and Karen, tolerated my frequent incursions into their home to use their computer to create the manuscript.

Dr. John Hyson transported me to the National Archives on several occasions and introduced me to their inner workings. Mr. Mitchell Yockelson, Archivist at the Archives, was very helpful in locating the records of the Army Signal School, and in the reproduction of maps and other material. Luther Hanson of the Army Quartermaster Museum in Fort Lee, Virginia, Dr. Dan Zimmerman of the Fort Dix Museum, and Dolores Opplinger of the Signal Corps Museum, Fort Gordon, Georgia, helped me locate an illustration of the Signal Corps patch. Thomas Proffitt of the Army Institute of Heraldry and Colonel David Kyle were of considerable help in forwarding to me copies of December, 1918 orders describing different shoulder patches for unattached First Army personnel. Dr. Richard Sommers and Randy Hackenburg, of the U.S. Army Military History Institute in Carlisle Barracks, Pa. provided support and helped in the reproduction of material I had previously donated. My editor, Dr. Martin Gordon, has given helpful advice and guidance to a neophyte author. Dr. Clara Heyn, some of whose family suffered greatly at the hands of Nazi Germany, was of assistance to me in reading the original manuscript and making some corrections in the German grammar. George Voellmer was also helpful in this regard. My good friend, Richard Hart, has been of invaluable assistance, helping with corrections and advice.

My other two children, Clare and Robert Hinrichs, also encouraged their father's endeavors in retirement. Last, but by no means least, my good wife, Susanne, has been very supportive and helpful throughout this whole endeavor.

Ernest H. Hinrichs, Jr.
August 8, 1995

INTRODUCTION

In the case of the foot soldier, wars are usually chronicled through the medium of letters written home to families and friends. Some soldiers do keep journals, but this is unusual, and I suspect many of these are lost to history upon the veterans' demise. Field grade officers and generals will write memoirs and books and these are important additions to the historical record. But it is rare for an enlisted man to keep a journal and rarer still for him to put his account into book form. It is unfortunate but true that much valuable historical material lies in attics and trunks and is eventually lost.

Listening In is the product of two epochal events in American history, the first World War and the great depression of 1932. In his early years my father had kept a journal and he continued this habit after he was drafted in 1917. After the war he became a dentist, graduating from the dental school of the University of Maryland in 1925. When he started to practice dentistry, the work on this book, originally titled *Listening Post*, was begun, but languished until the depression came, which cut down on his patient load and provided time to work on the book in the office.

Born on November 16, 1891, my father spent his early years in what is now the Reservoir Hill area of Baltimore. His mother's family lived on an estate that comprised a present day city block. His maternal grandfather, George Wilhelm Gail, had come from Giessen, Germany in the early nineteenth century, having been sent to America to buy tobacco for his father's tobacco factory. Making many connections in the German American community, he proceeded to begin the manufacture of tobacco in Baltimore, which gradually became a most successful business, particularly in the era after the Civil War. George Wilhelm Gail had learned English while still in Germany, and was fluent, but in the house and in the Hinrichs family, German was spoken among family members.

My grandfather, John Hinrichs, died in 1912. He was more scholarly and less practical than my great-grandfather Gail. The Hinrichs family had been in the dry goods business in Baltimore during the Civil War. In the early 1900's John Hinrichs published bland volumes of cable code words, used in international trade. Being a great admirer of Rudyard Kipling, he placed a quotation from Kipling's poem "The Deep Sea Cables" on the title page. My father had a first cousin on the Hinrichs side, Alfred Fadé, an American citizen who joined the Kaiser's Army as a lieutenant in 1915 and was killed when twenty years old at Château Thierry in July 1918. It was not only in the American Civil War that relatives fought each other.

Ernest Hinrichs attended Friends School in what is now the Bolton Hill area of Baltimore, not far from the Hinrichs residence on the corner of the Gail estate. Around the time of graduation he became ill with rheumatic fever. He was treated by the well-known cardiologist from Johns Hopkins, Dr. William Thayer, and was confined to a darkened room for an extended period. Starting with the engineering class of 1914 at Hopkins, he was forced by his illness to drop back to the class of 1917. The break due to illness had caused scheduling difficulties in his courses and he again dropped out in November 1915. In January 1916 he went to work for the Chesapeake and Potomac Telephone company of Baltimore in the traffic department. In his journal for the year 1916 there are many references to the military situation in Europe, which in some ways foreshadow some of the comments made in *Listening In*.

In the text of the book there are numerous references to aviation activity. One of the reasons was that my father was a frustrated aviator. He had been an avid builder of flying model airplanes and photographed Hubert Latham flying the Antoinette mono-plane at Halethorpe, Maryland in 1910. Latham flew over Baltimore to capture a $5000 prize offered by *The Baltimore Sun*. At one point my father built a full size glider, but he was unable to make the first flight before he was hospitalized. One of his brothers attempted to fly it from a big hill in front of the Baltimore Country Club, resulting in a crash. In the summer of 1915 my father went to Newport News, Virginia for his first airplane flight, a trip around its harbor in a Curtis Flying Boat. In 1917 he applied for the Air Service and failed the depth perception test.

While on the Bay Steamer during his trip to Newport News for the flying boat flight, my father encountered Carl Luederitz, the German Consul in Baltimore who had been a friend of his father's. He was invited to go aboard the *Prinz Eitel Friederich*, a German Raider that was interned in Newport News. He also went aboard the German cargo submarine *Deutschland* which came to Baltimore in 1916. It is of interest that in the accounts in my father's journal in the year 1916 the term Teutons instead of Germans is frequently encountered in descriptions of the fighting in Europe. He was very much aware that he was of German extraction, from both sides of his family. He had voted for Woodrow Wilson in 1916, supporting him because of the fourteen points that Wilson had set forth.

I remember one anecdote that illustrates this point. Early in World War II a cartoon appeared in the *Saturday Evening Post* which showed an ancient Confederate Civil War veteran raging in a wheelchair. The caption was: "If Pickett had charged five minutes earlier at Gettysburg there never would have been any Hitler!" My father's reaction was "That's not funny. That is true." His contention was that if the South had won the Civil War a divided United States would never have been able to supply meaningful assistance to the Allies in World War I, and there would have been no Versailles treaty. He believed that the Versailles treaty and punitive war reparations imposed by the Allied powers, which resulted in massive inflation in postwar Germany, were the principal causes of the rise of Nazism and World War II. In the period preceding the war, he gave several talks to the Lions Club of North Baltimore in which he anticipated the dismemberment of Czechoslovakia and the abolition of the Polish Corridor. He felt that Germany was the geocentric center of Europe. In a discussion with my uncle, who was married to a British subject, he anticipated the Russo-German pact of 1939 that gave Hitler a freer hand in Poland. His insight into the European situation in the 1930's was incisive and not always the popular one. I well remember that he was furious at the time of the Yalta conference when most of eastern Europe was turned over to the Soviet Union, and supported Paul Nitze, another cousin, in his attitude toward the Soviets and the cold war.

It was because of sentiments such as these in an earlier day that my father often quoted the French soldiers he was with in the area around Pexonne, France in April and May of 1918: "Quelle guerre! Quelle stupidité!"

Ernest H. Hinrichs, Jr.
December 1992

Taken at Dornholzhausen, Hinrichs' summer home in Germany, in the summer of 1908. Left to right are, John Hinrichs, Ernest Hinrichs' older brother; Ernest Hinrichs, standing; and then seated, Ernest Hinrichs' father, John Hinrichs; younger brother Paul; and his uncle Paul C. Hinrichs. The older Paul Hinrichs had been born in Baltimore but had returned to Germany to live. In 1933 two stained glass windows which he donated were dedicated in the Zion Church, located on the Plaza in Baltimore, Maryland, opposite City Hall.

Part I

Chapter 1

"Un Bon Secteur"

Pexonne and Chasseur "Post D'Écoute"

After the Zimmerman Telegram and the Telefunken Affair, the war drums in America beat louder than ever. German-Americans were derisively referred to as "hyphenates." Anti-German sentiment and suspicion increased, culminating in the lynching of a coal miner of German extraction in Collinsville, Illinois, in the early morning hours of April 5, 1918.[1] My father wrote several letters to the editor of the Baltimore Sun in 1916. Not all were mailed, but nevertheless were copied into his journal. The last entry in my father's journal before he left for military service reads as follows:

November 6th, 1917.

I'm a rookie. Am now in the pay of Uncle Sam as Private Hinrichs. The machinery of the Draft has done its work and tomorrow I leave for Camp Meade to begin my training as a soldier. Who would have thought when this war began that my life would finally come under its influence? The thing has grown bigger and bigger until it has become all absorbing. No man can live his life as he pleases. All are subject to the baneful influence of the greatest struggles of history. Mankind is on edge and the world has gone topsy-turvy. No man is certain of his future. We are now inextricably tied up with the Allied cause. Their fortune is our fortune. Accordingly, we must exert ourselves. Each man has become simply a unit in the organism of the nation. It is as though the nation as a whole had suddenly become the animal and the individual simply a red corpuscle in its veins. When I am ordered I obey. "Theirs not to reason why."

As soon as I was accepted by the examining physician I went right over to Washington and put in my application for the flying service. As yet I have heard nothing, but I am hoping that I will be transferred from the Infantry to the Aviation section before long. How long will I be at Camp Meade? What has the next year in store for me?

3

Perilous and uncertain times, these! No man can be sure of food and bed for the coming years. The only sure thing a man possesses is his education.

The next entry in my father's journal is July 15, 1919. He reported to the Towson, Maryland courthouse on November 7, 1917, and was placed in Company D of the 313th Infantry Regiment of the 79th Division at Meade.[2] Corporal Hinrichs was one of two men picked from the 40,000 men at the post and sent to Camp Vaile, New Jersey for training in Radio Intelligence because of German fluency. His ship sailed from New Jersey on March 20th, 1918. He was shortly sent to a French School at Langres, France for further training.

On November 7, 1917, Ernest Hinrichs stands in a group of new draftees in front of the County Courthouse in Towson, Maryland, awaiting transportation to Camp Meade. The building is still the seat of Baltimore County government.

April 28, 1918.

I sit at the table ten feet underground, listening. All the others, three Frenchmen and one American, sleep. Our electric light has stopped working. I write by a single flickering candle and the dim lights of the amplifier. On a chair beside me is my pistol belt. My gas mask and tin hat are slung across the back of the chair. A box of dirty grenades stands against a post.

Listening from 2 to 6 A.M. From the telephone receiver on one ear the ground noises roar and crackle. These are static and generator disturbances common to the trench listening set. Into the other ear comes only the sound of an occasional flare shot to illuminate no-man's land, the crack of a nervous sentry's rifle or the faint rustle of the wind in the trees outside.

Late fall 1917, at Camp Meade, Maryland. After war was declared, these barracks were constructed in the summer of 1917, on land newly purchased from the Washington, Baltimore, and Annapolis Railroad.

3 A.M.—the flares are becoming more frequent. Rat—tat—tat, a machine gun is added to the other noises. The patch of black sky at the end of the four foot tunnel westward, which serves for a window, is illuminated as by a distant lightning flash; 1, 2, 3, 4, 5, seconds, a dull thud, then the peculiar swishing sound of a heavy shell passing over followed by a terrific explosion that jars dirt down my neck from the log ceiling.

A noise in the ear phone. I pull the head set over both ears and strain to catch it. Talk, indistinct German? No, French—"A droit! Quatre-vingt meters bas!" etc. I cannot make it out, so go over and shake D'Anglard. He jumps up and puts on his head set. His eyes open as he listens.

"It is the French Artillery observer," he says, "but he is not using code. It is against the rules." He grabs a pencil and writes rapidly. Another flash to the west is followed by a heavy explosion over the hill.

"A gauche! Dix-sept metres—haut quarante—." There is more voluble French over the wire, then silence. D'Anglard scribbles hurriedly.

"He should not spot gun fire from the front lines without code. He will be reported."

Maurice D'Anglard speaks in English because he has been a motorcycle pacemaker in the States. In 1914 he joined the Foreign Legion and fought in it for over a year. The French chose him for this service because of his German. We are here to get information from the enemy and also to prevent the enemy from getting information from us. We are to police our own lines. Telephone conversation in the trenches is forbidden except in emergency because such conversation has a way of leaking across no-man's land to the enemy listening stations, which are as well organized as we are.

4 A.M.—The night continues calm. D'Anglard has gone back to bed. There is plenty of time to write, and too much time to think. We are supposed to give all our attention to the job of listening, but you can't keep your attention fixed hour

The construction of trenches and revetments, as would be needed by 79th Division in France, was practiced at Meade.

This crew at Camp Meade has constructed a log dugout as would be needed in France.

after hour on a roaring buzz and banging static. Everybody is asleep. It is so lonesome I must keep myself awake by recording my thoughts. Sometimes I think I am dreaming. It is all so unreal, fantastic. What a strange succession of events has drawn through all the outer currents of the whirlpool into the vortex of this war which seems to be gathering in all mankind. Six months ago a peaceful clerk at a desk in the traffic engineer's office of the C. and P. Telephone Company, Baltimore. Of German stock—before I went to school I spoke German better than English—raised in a large family, according to German customs and family traditions—to this end. Strange that the German in me should have been the reason for my sudden transfer, without explanation, out of the 313th Infantry after six weeks at Camp Meade, to Camp Vaile, New Jersey and the Signal Corps. One other man, a Dutchman, who later claimed Dutch citizenship, and myself, were picked out of the 40,000 men at Camp Meade. We do not know why. My company said that they knew only that orders had come through from Washington transferring me to Little Silver, New Jersey.

When we got off the train at Little Silver, a Signal Corps Sergeant came up to us and said:

"You Pigeon Men?"

A camp scene, showing life in quarters at Camp Meade in November 1917.

Taken at Camp Vaile, New Jersey, later renamed Fort Monmouth. The soldier on the right is named Lipps, others are unknown. For this first month nothing was accomplished, but by February, there were intensive classes in military German.

We stared at him blankly. "Know anything about Pigeons?" We had to confess that we did not. "Speak German?" We admitted it rather reluctantly. "This way." He piled us, barracks bags and all, into a truck.

I was at Camp Vaile for two months; winter months that passed so slowly and now seem but a moment. Daily they came in, by twos and threes, from every state in the Union—German speaking telephone men and wireless operators. For a month we sat around and did nothing, then came classes in military German followed by secret examinations in which we were tested as to our ability to understand German over the telephone. Those of us who passed were placed on the overseas list without further instruction.

It was not until we arrived at the signal school at Langres, France that we got any idea of what this listening business involved. Then they tried in two weeks to cram into us the whole theory and practice of wireless telegraphy. For six hours each night we were put on the wireless intercept stations and we spent every spare hour during the day at buzzer practice. Code, everything was code, and the time was so short.[3] It had been just three weeks ago that our transport had docked at St. Nazaire and there I was, green in the arts of war to say the least, and very thankful to have the French of this service to

Trainees at Camp Vaile, New Jersey. Left to right are Hinrichs, Mathes, Mahonay, and Waters. By chance, Hinrichs met Waters years later in a cafeteria in Baltimore.

guide me. "Un bon secteur" and they ought to know; most of them have been in the war since the beginning. We had to set up our receivers alongside of theirs and to learn the intricacies of this listening game from them.

5 A.M. Dawn is coming. I have this head set on for three hours and am dog tired. Most of the time the static has been heavy and sometimes most unpleasant. D'Anglard is supposed to be listening at the French apparatus, but he said that there was no use in us both listening, so he has gone to sleep. I'll turn it over to him now and crawl in myself.

18 — LANGRES. — Quartier Turenne. — LL.

My father arrived in France in late March or early April of 1918. He was shortly afterward sent to this school run by the French Army in Langres, France for two weeks of intensive training in wireless telegraphy. He was not transferred out of this school until May 3, 1918, after having been sent to Pexonne.

The author drew this sketch of Pexonne from a postcard.

PEXONNE. - La Gare

The railroad station in Pexonne, three miles from the front.

On the back of this postcard, the author had written: "Dear Old Pexonne. Note the manure piles. More wrecked later. View away from front."

April 30, 1918 (Two days later, written at our rest quarters at Pexonne, three miles behind the lines.)

At present we are to be on post forty-eight hours and off forty-eight hours. During our off hours we can go where we please in the lines on our pass. I have certainly seen a lot in these first few days at the front.

The first day.

We slept the night of April 24th on the floor of the headquarters building in Baccarat. Eight miles from the lines, Baccarat is the headquarters of the U.S. forty-second Division. This division is also known as the Rainbow because its individual regiments come from states in different parts of the Union. I presented my papers to the Division Intelligence Officer. The town was packed with troops and the billeting officer could find no place for us. Next morning we piled into two Ford trucks. There were eight men, each with a full pack, tin hat, gas mask, side arms, and a barrack bag. It was raining of course. It usually does over here.

I shall never forget my first impression of Pexonne. We knew we were approaching the lines by the increasing amount of camouflaged screening along the road, and the artillery emplacements. Pexonne was the first village that showed unmistakable signs of wreckage. It is a sleepy little agricultural town. There is the usual central square with a steepled church at the far end; ancient stone buildings, half barn and half dwelling; two large stone water troughs at which bent peasant women are ever busy washing clothes. There is life of all kinds: civilians and troops, both French and American. Also cows, horses, dogs, chickens, goats, pigs, and manure piles.

FENNEVILLER

On the reverse of this postcard, my father had written: "A little bit of a place just in front of Pexonne. The road forward ran through here. Boche made it unhealthy often. Nothing much left now."

We drew up before our new quarters, an old three story stone building at the end of the town. This place is comfortable enough. Of course every window has been smashed long ago and a shell has gone through the roof, but the house is still sufficiently solid to live in and there is a reinforced cellar that looks good to me. I got a bed in what was formerly the kitchen. It is the best in the place, a wooden frame with wire stretched across the top and a straw mattress. Everything would be perfect if it were not for the fleas. These pesky creatures take to me in particular. When they begin their evening meal they set me on fire. Someone has said, "You pay the 'cooties'' traveling expenses but the fleas' board bill."

This kitchen, called "The Non-Coms Club," is on the southwest corner of the house. D'Anglard, the big Frenchman, immediately pointed out that it was the best and safest room in the house, away from the enemy and on the ground floor, with electric light and a view into the garden. They have given it to us because we are their guests and in their charge for instruction. Israel, Treubel, Keller and I now occupy it. When we go on post four others come in. The first night after we returned from supper at the headquarters mess uptown, there was a meeting in this room, we eight Americans and as many French. None of us could speak French and not many French knew English, but we had no trouble at all in getting acquainted. There was a common language between us—German.

Presently the French Sergeant "Chef du Groupe" came in. He was dressed up like an officer, spick and span with tailor made uniform, black leather leggings and polished shoes. A good looking chap; black hair, clean shaven, sparkling eyes and a broad grin. He made a little speech of welcome in the purest German. He was an Alsatian, no doubt, and a product of German occupation, as are most of these men.

There was a commotion at the door and a man entered with a case of beer which he placed on the floor between the bunks. When every man had a bottle and the noise had subsided we drank to "Les Americans," "The French" and to the "Fraternity P.T.B."[4] Then the Sergeant clapped his hands for quiet and at last became serious. "Gentlemen, this is a very happy occasion. I am sorry that it must be cut short. Light must be out by nine o'clock and it is now eight-thirty. You can draw lots for posts and then go to bed, for all must be up at six to prepare to leave for the lines."

The second day.

The French routed us out at daybreak. The night had passed peacefully enough; there were only a few distant gun reports and the fleas were still somewhat shy. At the headquarters mess I filled my pack with my share of eats for two days. The Frenchmen were waiting for us before the house when we returned.

I had drawn the Chasseur position and was immediately taken in tow by D'Anglard, Pompie and Corporal DuBois, otherwise known as "Papa DuBois." By the way, if these names sound rather queer, I am told they are assumed by these men because they do not wish by any chance to be identified by the Germans in case of capture. Being Alsatians they would be considered traitors to the German cause.

We set off on the highway leading out of Pexonne to the northeast. It takes us through a very badly battered part of the town. The ground here must have been hotly contested in 1914, when the Germans swept in and took possession of all the land back to Baccarat. There is not one house left upright, just a mass of broken walls. A church with a little cemetery is hardly recognizable; there are already big bushes growing in the interior.

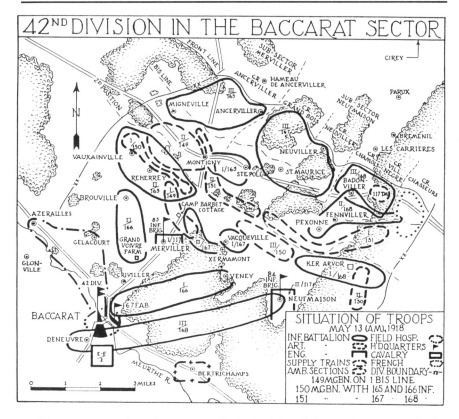

42ND DIVISION IN THE BACCARAT SECTOR

SITUATION OF TROOPS
MAY 13 (A.M.) 1918
INF. BATTALION — FIELD HOSP.
ART. — H'DQUARTERS
ENG. — CAVALRY
SUPPLY TRAINS — FRENCH
AMB. SECTIONS — DIV. BOUNDARY
149 MG.BN. ON 1 BIS LINE
150 MG.BN. WITH 165 AND 166 INF.
151 " " 167 · 168 ·

We pass on out into the country. On both sides of the road are camouflaging fences of pine boughs hung on wires forming screens ten feet high, and every hundred yards a piece of green and brown daubed cloth is stretched across overhead like a portiere. We traverse about three kilometers of this road and come into a town that is almost completely wrecked. It is Badonvillers, a bigger place than Pexonne. It is now full of troops of the forty-second Division. The civilians have left. The soldiers are quartered in the cellars and first floors reinforced with sandbags, logs and stones. We turn east into the main street. At three or four points there are barricades on the sides of the way with a barbed wire obstacle ready to place in the road opening. The town hall is a mass of ruins and every house on the square before it is a shell.

Continuing our way we reach the last barricade. Here we must show our passes to a sentry. Beyond the town the road is not screened but runs through a valley up toward the hills. A large stone mill sits squarely in the middle of the pass and there are evidences of a hot fight.

The field nearby is now a cemetery with fully five hundred crosses. Barbed wire is all along the road. Entanglements are everywhere and in the most unexpected places, some old and rusted and some new.

Just beyond the mill there is an American Red Cross station to the left of the road, a very neat place dug into the bank. The road turns to the right and the embankment on the left is covered with bomb-proofs and dugouts full of U.S. troops. The place is called "Village Nègre."

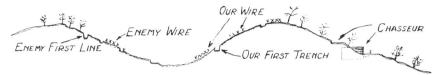

We now leave the main road, taking a fork to the right. In the tongue are the graves of five French and three German officers. Our route takes us down the hill and over a little brook to the other side of the valley. We strike up a path through the woods. The ascent becomes steep; it climbs perhaps three hundred feet and then comes out on the main road which here runs parallel with the front on the lea side of a hill so that it is hidden from the enemy.

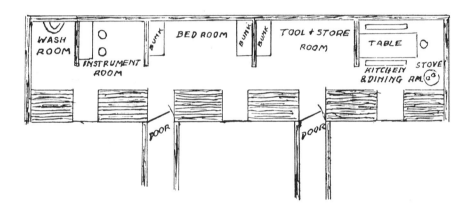

The Chasseur dugout is built into the side of the hill and to the right of the road. It is in the middle of an open forest which has not been shot to pieces very much. The roof is six feet of logs and earth and the front wall at least four feet thick. The hill protects us from direct view from the enemy so that we can come out into the open safely.

Maurice D'Anglard immediately becomes enthusiastic about the good points of the "Chasseur, Poste D'Écoute."

"It is a wonderful dugout, the best in the line; strong and dry, warm in winter and cool in summer, with washroom, workroom, bedroom, tool room and kitchenette dining room."

He ushers us proudly from one room to another.

"We have electric light and running water."

He leads us into the washroom, where the trickle of a spring has been run into a basin.

Then I become interested in the listening apparatus. What a different thing this is than we had pictured in the States. Vaguely we had imagined ourselves covered with mud, crouching in a shell hole with a microphone [sic] to our ear. It was not a pleasant image and we brushed it out of our minds, only to have it creep back and haunt us after lights were out and the January wind whistled through the cracked barracks room window.

Sometimes the foreboding returns. There is no end to this war. To the north the Germans move forward daily. We are here for training only.[5] Who can tell where I will be a few months from now?

Here, instead of lying in a mud hole, we sit before a three bulb amplifier of special design.[6] Insulated wires run forward through the trenches and out into no-man's land. They are grounded as close to the enemy trenches as possible. The French also use the "Loop," an unbroken wire that runs through no-man's land parallel to the trenches for perhaps a quarter of a mile and then back to the receiver.[7] They claim that there is less static and ground noise with the "Loop," but it is easily broken by shell fire.[8]

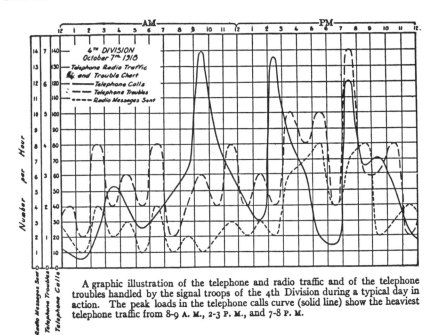

A graphic illustration of the telephone and radio traffic and of the telephone troubles handled by the signal troops of the 4th Division during a typical day in action. The peak loads in the telephone calls curve (solid line) show the heaviest telephone traffic from 8-9 A. M., 2-3 P. M., and 7-8 P. M.

From the Fourth Division 1920.

I sit with the receiver on my ear for a half hour and there is nothing but a great deal of noise and static. I am beginning to get discouraged when suddenly I hear a signal: Da—ti—Da—ti—ti—ti—ti—Da—Da—Da—ti, etc.

"Pompie," sitting beside me, explains in German:

"It is the American station above Village Nègre. They test every two hours. Now comes the return."

Ti—Da—Da—Ti——

There is a pause of another ten minutes with my ear beginning to ache from the banging and cracking in the receiver. Then the Frenchman leans forward intently. I had heard nothing, but as he began to write, it came to me also, far away, thin and high pitched:

U M—U M—pause—U M—U M—pause—U M—U M—V A S—A S—P Q—P Q—W P G—W P G.

A pause. Pompie looks up, winks and whispers: "Station P.Q. will answer. The Boche test lines." Presently it came, louder and more distinct:

U M—U M—P Q—P Q—N F—N F—M G—M G.

Pompie copies it down. Everything heard must be written in the daily report to Headquarters Intelligence, where I am told that code experts have no difficulty in deciphering the messages. The reports from all along the line give valuable information.

"Is there no telephone conversation?" I ask.

"Ah!" sighs Pompie. "Now we seldom hear the Boche talk. They know we listen and are discreetly silent, but let things become active—a push or a raid." His eyes dance wisely and he pats the instrument affectionately.

"Sometimes they talk."

The third day. April 28th.

During the early hours when I was at the receiver, French high explosive shells began to sail by unpleasantly close overhead. They landed out front, one or two a little short, and our wires were broken.

I was aroused from sleep by the smiling Pompie who stood over me with a cup of black coffee in one hand and a bottle of Cognac in the other.

"Raus! Kaffee! Nehmen Sie Cognac?" (Out! Coffee! Do you take Cognac?)

Not waiting for a reply, he strengthened the coffee out of the bottle and handed me the cup and a big slice of black French bread.

"Pompie" is a nickname meaning Fireman. He was a strapping fellow, only twenty-two. Until recently he had been serving in the Paris Fire Department. His home and family were in Strasburg, back of the German lines and he had not seen them since the war began. A great boy; I had known him only two days but I felt as though I had grown up with him. He had strong regular features, with pink cheeks and wonderful teeth. He was not very tall, but was massive in the shoulders and chest. His face was honest and open with an unquenchable smile that kept that row of pearls in his mouth always shining. Thinking of his troubles, with his parents within the German lines, I certainly admired his spirit. In fact, I felt that we must hand it to all of these Frenchmen, for the way they laughed after almost four years of war.

"Der Draht ist zerrissen," was his next statement. He looked at me doubtfully.

"Ich geh' raus, gehen Sie mit?"

Would I go with him and help him fix the wire? I dipped that hard black bread into the doped coffee while Pompie waited, grinning. With such a face looking at me, what could I do but grin back?

* *

We go up over the hill following our wire through muddy trenches. Pompie is in front with a bag of lineman's tools. We carry a pole between us on which is mounted a big spool of telephone wire. There is a sign "Boyau de Rendez-vous." We turn down this trench and zigzag forward nearer and nearer the Boche lines through obstacles and entanglements. There are tunnels and lookout points with rifle loop holes. Finally it comes out on the side of a little valley on the other slope of which is the Boche line. The trench runs on down the hill and we follow the wire down it. Presently we come

We go up _____

In all likelihood, my father drew this sketch of a wire laying party after the war.

upon a corporal and a squad in a very strong position. It is the French "Petite Poste." Sentries are ever watchful, looking through slits, with machine guns ready poised.

We set down our burden and Pompie has a consultation with the corporal. The corporal picks out one of his men and leads the way into an abandoned trench where a great mass of tangled barbed wire fills the path. Our wires pass under the obstacle. We begin laboriously to work our way through, pushing the spool before us, now on our stomachs and in the mud, now hastily up and over. It takes us fully ten minutes to negotiate that fifty feet of "barbele," as the French call it.

We are entering that accursed strip of land extending from the Swiss border to the sea between the contending armies; the loneliest and most desolate place in the world; full of rusting wire and rotting equipment of all kinds and barren and pock marked as though by the plague. My wrist watch says 11 A.M. The sun stands high in the heavens and I wonder a little that we are out in the daylight, but Pompie and the corporal are matter of fact and their composure is reassuring. In silence we proceed, stooping low in the dilapidated ditch, climbing over debris and in and out of shell holes, always following the wire.

We had gone perhaps a hundred yards when Pompie turned in a deep spot where we could almost stand upright without showing ourselves. We set the pole crosswise in the ditch to form an axle for the spool to revolve on. The corporal and his man stood watch while we prepared to run our line.

Pompie went off down a side ditch with the end of the wire. I kept the wire unrolling and free from snags. It was slow work. The further away he went the slower we progressed. The ditch was tortuous and full of debris. An immense amount of wire had unrolled and still it dragged out jerkily. I became fascinated watching that wire. Every time it stopped I thought that was all, and then it would creep forward again, pulling out taut like an earthworm with the strain of its movement. Pompie had been out of sight close to an hour. I was beginning to wonder when this would end. The silence was oppressive, only an occasional gun report in the distance and high overhead the hum of a plane.

Suddenly—CRACK!—a single rifle shot in the German line. The sound echoed up and down the valley. Pompie? Had they seen him? In my anxiety I stood up to peep forward over the edge of the ditch. The corporal pulled me down and brushed by me, stooping low, his eyes on the wire which had stopped moving. He paused, hand on wire, as though listening. Another report! I looked up just in time to see a tin-can-like object with fins out back describe a wide arc. It landed with a heavy explosion about two hundred feet out. Almost at the same moment Pompie came tumbling around the corner of the ditch. To my amazement he was grinning from ear to ear.

"Fertig! Zurück!"

He motioned us back as he pulled out his pliers, cut the new wire and the old wire, and began to peel the insulation. We started back, the corporal's man taking the other end of the spool pole. We had not gone a hundred feet before Pompie joined us. The return was made without incident, although there was increased firing from both sides.*

* * * * * * * * * * * * * * * *

At the Chasseur we found Lieutenant Thompson who has charge of us with Captain Hulburt** who was making some experiments with the apparatus. The French invited them to stay for dinner. They could not resist the smell of nicely done steak and "pomme de terre frites." They knew it was beneath the dignity of officers to eat with enlisted men, but as soon as we sat down all rank was forgotten and we had a jolly party.

Imagine a rough timber room, about ten feet square and very crowded. A little cook stove was in one corner emitting much smoke, which slowly found its way out the four foot tunnel of a window. In the corner opposite the stove there was a big stack of wood; in the third corner was the door and the fourth held a dozen wine bottles. Fill this space with a table, two benches, a stool and six men and you get an idea of what it was like.

This was a stranger dinner than the mad tea party. Two young and newly made American officers, two raw U.S. rookies, and two Frenchmen, both with three years service behind them. Standing before the stove was Papa DuBois, flourishing a cooking fork and wiping onion tears while he bowed the officers to their seats on the bench furthest from the stove, where there was less heat and smoke. He was host, cook, waiter, and entertainer. Fifty-one years old, possessor of the Médaille Militaire and Croix de Guerre with three palm leaves and a star, he is at liberty to retire when he wishes. Short and wiry with a grizzly beard, beady black eyes and a round bald head, he is wonderfully active and energetic, and I have never seen anyone eat with such enthusiasm.

Notes: (In longhand and probably added at a later date)
* It is very evident to me now that the Germans had not seen Pompie. I know now that, if they had spotted us out there, they would have made it most unpleasant for us.
* * Eddy Hulbert of Baltimore.

Lieutenant Thompson began to question him about his war experiences, but he was reticent and his mouth was full of potatoes. It was not until the Pinard (vin rouge) had gone around the third time that they got him started and he switched from French into the more familiar German.

"Ach! This first palm was nothing. It was early in the war and I had escaped when the others were killed. I did not deserve it. But this one," he pointed to the second palm leaf, "it was almost the end of me."

"It was a very dark night and we were running a wire into their lines. We did not have amplifiers then and ran our wires right in. We had reached the second trench and had seen no one, when suddenly we bumped right into a German outpost. Oi! Everything went off at once. I stumbled and fell and the others got ahead. At the entanglement I was caught and could not pull loose."

He stuck out his right hand and pointed to a mean scar in the flesh between the thumb and first finger.

"The barbs did that; two got in there and whichever way I pulled they went deeper. The grenades! Ooh!" He rolled his eyes, bit his tongue and let out a howl like a dog. "Right at my back they went off. I thought my last hour had come."

"Lasst mich nicht hier! Um Gottes willen, lasst mich nicht hier!" (Don't leave me here! For God's sake, don't leave me here!) I cried loudly after the others and then more terrible explosions and I remember no more."

He stopped as though the story were finished. Then he reached for the wine bottle, poured himself another cup and leaned back in his seat with his eyes closed.

"But you are here. You got away," probed the Lieutenant.

"I died on the wire; a slow horrible death as the grenades whipped my back to pieces." Suddenly he arose, wheeled around, and with a quick motion jerked his shirt up over his head. We gasped at the sight that met our eyes. His back was a mass of mutilated flesh. There was not a piece of skin the size of a silver dollar which was not scarred.

"One hundred and nine pieces of metal they picked out of me," he went on. "Three months I lay between life and death and for ten months I was an invalid. Later they told me that Siebert, my good comrade, Siebert, who is dead now, had come back and released me. At the risk of his life he had carried me into our lines although he thought I was a corpse."

Suddenly his expression changed. He smiled and drew up his shoulders in an expressive shrug. "C'est la guerre!" he exclaimed. "But this is a tough old carcass; it still does very well, and if it does not last so very much longer—." He shrugged again as though to say "nothing matters."

After dinner, the officers left us to visit the next post up the line to the north. There are three listening posts in this group. They are given fanciful names by the French: Le Hussard, Le Dragon, Le Chasseur. The personnel of these stations are known as the Fraternity P. T. B. Exactly what the letters mean I have not been able to find out. One Frenchman says, "Poste Telephone Boche"; another immediately contradicts him and makes it "Poste Telephone Battalion." But it matters little; the peculiar thing about the P. T. B. service and personnel is that it is an organization entirely outside of the line battalion, regiment or division. Our company organization is at Toul, sixty miles away. Our mail address is Radio Intelligence G. H. Q.* Lieutenant Thompson

---

* Note: (Handwritten by Author) This was later changed to Radio Section S. C. G. H. Q.

Toul, where company headquarters of the radio service personnel was located.

says he will come around every two weeks with our letters. Well, it looks like we won't be bothered with any "Shave Tails" in this outfit anyway and most of the time we will be our own bosses.

At about 8 P.M. our relief arrived. We packed up our things and started back toward Pexonne. We were approaching Village Nègre when somebody hailed us. I looked around and there was Johnny Mealy of Mount Washington, a suburb of Baltimore, standing in a dugout doorway. We talked a few minutes and he said: "There are a lot of fellows here that you know; it's the 117th trench mortar battery." This was part of the Rainbow Division. He led me in and there were several other familiar faces including Dick Holmes from Hopkins and the Brawner boys from Roland Park. It was a regular homecoming and I have felt better ever since. They showed us their mortar positions and the "flying Pigs" they use for ammunition.

I am writing this at the French window of the Non-Coms club in Pexonne. There is an unusual amount of racket outside. I am going out and see what's up.

Ten minutes later.

The Boche antiaircraft guns were firing at two groups of Allied bombing planes on their way back from a raid. They crossed over into Germany at six o'clock this morning, now it is eleven. The roar of their motors is still in my ears. When I went out, six planes in "V" formation were just coming out from behind a cloud. Little black and white puffs of bursting shrapnel speckled the sky. They dodged right into another big cloud to escape the barrage. I thought that was all and then five more appeared a little to the south and sped across the strip of blue. There may have been six in this group when they went over this morning. An inspiring sight. It's hard to realize that human beings are seated in those graceful birds playing hide and seek among the clouds. Except for the roar of their motors, they might very well be taken for a flock of geese.

In the yard, the French have put up a horizontal bar. As I write, two young fellows have been doing stunts to the accompaniment of a continual flow of words. These men talk too fast for me. They run words into each other and cut sentences in the middle, so that the little French I know doesn't help a bit. They soon got tired of the bar and, still, having surplus energy to work off this fine spring day, looked around for other amusement.

Now they are going through mock artillery maneuvers and the noise of the command and the racket the "gun" makes has drawn everybody out to watch. They have wired a six foot length of stovepipe across an old pushcart axle and wheels. Two other Frenchmen have joined the game. The four of them wheel the gun into position. One points it, another places a tin can in the breach, and at the word of command from the crew captain, my friend Pompie gives it a whack with a stick that sends the can flying out the other end of the pipe and fifty feet across the yard. With a vibrant word of command, the gun is whirled to a new position facing the crowd in the doorway, and a rapid fire of "shells" is released, scattering the onlookers amid much merriment. There is plenty of ammunition, for all France is now covered with corn-willy cans. They have a name for this artillery but I dare not repeat it.

Now they have a new idea. They have tied a wire to a can and dropped it into the gun muzzle. Other cans are put in on top of this one until the pipe is full. Pompie carries the wire around a little tree and back to the gun. At command, Pompie pulls the wire with all his might. The result is a hail of can "shrapnel" at the tree with much laughter.

Chapter 2

Wireless and T.P.S.

As I studied this manuscript, one thing that impressed me as a World War II veteran with some infantry basic training was the fact that some combat service support troops in World War I were apparently sent overseas with very little training in warfare. The fact that World War I was primarily thought of as trench warfare, with little of the fluidity of World War II, may have been one reason for this. Though my father was in the 313th Infantry regiment at Camp Meade for six weeks, his training in gas warfare seems to have been sparse. He had never thrown a hand grenade when he went to France and he was issued a Colt .45 with six shells but apparently had been given no pistol training.

In the text of this chapter it is obvious that my father believed that the Zeppelins were bombing London on the night of May 20, 1918. It is true that the airship was the primary strategic air weapon for Germany at the outset of World War I, but grievous losses soon caused a shift in Prussian military opinion. Graf Zeppelin himself came to support the development of very large aircraft. These had been used on the eastern front where Igor Sikorsky's "Ilia Mourmetz" giant bombers had bombed the Germans. Used first against the Russians, the R planes had a wingspan of around one hundred and forty feet with engines that were serviceable by mechanics while in flight. The raid on the night of May 19/20 was carried out by thirty-eight Gotha Bombers, three R planes, and two observation planes armed with a total of 14,550 kilograms of high explosives.[1] There were even thoughts of building bombers that would reach New York in 1919.

May 11, 1918.

What a wonderful thing is wireless. Here I sit underground in the line while into my ears pours the news of the warring capitals. There is no aerial, nothing to be seen to indicate a wireless station.* A very simple little box stands before me. In the top are three bulbs, very similar to ordinary electric light bulbs, which cast a dim light over my paper. From the box two wires run out into the trenches. That is all there is and yet we are able to catch all the latest press dispatches of the warring nations. All night long the air is full of messages. The great stations of France and Germany spit at each other at the appointed hour every night. There is a continual war argument going on, which at times assumes an almost humorous tone. At nine P.M. (10 in Germany) Nauen, Berlin has its say. Tonight it has been going steadily for over two hours. First the official German report, then press. We of this service are among the chosen few of the Allied countries who get the enemy dispatches at first hand and uncensored. This stuff never gets into the Allied papers and is frequently very interesting. At 1 A.M. the Eiffel tower has its say. It always comes back with a strong argument of rebuttal and gets in a few digs in return. So the aerial debate goes on. They frequently call each other liars and love to get sarcastic and spiteful. Sometimes it is very witty.

May 20th.

Keller, Treubel, and I were in the Non-Com Club this morning. We were discussing weighty problems of life, the strategy of war and international policies. This man Treubel has begun to interest me. He is a little fellow, very boyish in appearance. One would take him to be about twenty but he says he is twenty-four. With a round face, pink cheeks and blue eyes, he has all the earmarks of a Teuton and yet is so violently anti-German.

"These moonlight nights are fine for air raids," remarked Keller. "The wireless reports last night said the Zepps were over London again. That makes three times this week. I wonder just how much damage they did. Berlin made big claims but London denied it."

"Both sides probably lied as usual," said Treubel. "The Boche think they are scaring the English and they just make the English mad."

"A Zepp is a big target," continued Keller. "I don't see why they can't bring 'em down oftener than they do. London said one came down in flames, but the rest got away."

"A Zepp can be shot full of holes and still not come down," observed Treubel. "I saw one come back from a raid once with hundreds of holes in it."

He stopped and began oiling and rubbing the parts of his Colt .45 which he had all in pieces on his bunk. He takes this .45 apart every few days for the pleasure of putting it together again. It certainly does not get dirty from shooting. We got six shells each when the guns were given to us and two shots were all we dared spare for practice.

Keller and I both turned on Treubel. "How do you get that way? Where did you ever see a Zeppelin come down?"

"Well I did," insisted Treubel.

---

* Note: Remember, this was before the day of Radio Broadcasting.

"Yea, you did, same as you saw those five Germans with spiked helmets last week. You dreamed it." Keller spat on the floor in disgust.

Treubel concentrated on his gun, and as I looked at him a deeper flush spread over his face which I would have taken for shame at having been caught in a false-hood. But there was just the slightest tightening of the lips and drawing down of the brows that meant that there was another emotion struggling in that round head. Presently he undertook to justify his statement.

"In 1916, I was on the Dutch freighter *Rotterdam*. I was the wireless operator. She was torpedoed off Heligoland. The crew was picked up by a German fishing boat and landed at Hamburg. We were neutrals and given much freedom. I made friends with a fellow from the Zeppelin service and he took me out to the landing field."

He slid back the barrel of the reassembled Colt, leveled the gun at the stone floor and clicked the trigger. Was this a mere kid playing with a toy?

I remember one of the first days we were on the front when the French were much interested in our weapons and had expressed amazement at the size of our .45's. They had kidded Treubel and said that it would knock him over to shoot it. A beer bottle was put up on a stump and Treubel aimed at it from a distance of about six yards. To the surprise of us all, he hit it with the first bullet. He would not shoot again, laughed, and said that it was an accident and that he would rest on his honors.

May 25th.

We have been on the line one month today. After you get used to the idea of being under fire and the scenes and incidents of the front become commonplace, this war begins to be rather boring. At least here in Pexonne we lead a narrow existence. The one saving feature of this service is the variety produced by spending two days on post and then two days at Pexonne. This shift of scene keeps up the interest and prevents one from becoming utterly weary with the monotonous routine. The month has gone by with very little activity. The line remains exactly as it was when I arrived. The only development that I can see is the natural development, the difference be-tween the end of April and the end of May. The sun is shining warmer and more often and the green of spring spreads over the earth. With the good weather there has been an increase in the show in the air. The antiaircraft guns are always pounding away, but I have yet to see them hit anything.

Yesterday evening we went to the "movies." The Y.M.C.A. occupies one of the half house, half barn structures in town. Most of these houses are built that way, with cows, chickens, and pigs below and the family above. The "Y" runs a canteen down-stairs and upstairs is the auditorium. The doors are kept shut most of the time. Last night, it was worth your life to get into the place. When we arrived, a crowd of about a hundred men were already pounding at the closed barn door demanding admittance. As we waited, the mob swelled and became more impatient. After a while, the door swung in and since I was right in the stream opposite the entrance, the tide carried me through with my feet off the ground. Even the rafters were soon lined with men.

May 27th.

At the Chasseur again. A beautiful day, clear and warm. The Boche are absolutely silent. All artillery is taking a rest. Aeroplanes are as busy as ever, and every now and then the "Antis" pump lead into the sky. What goes up must come down. Yesterday on the way from Pexonne we were examining a couple of periscopes we found near Village Nègre. One was made of tin, very pretty to look at, but the mirrors were missing. Like this:

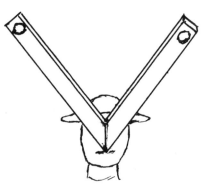

The other was a beauty. It had real glass in it, and even a lens or two. Here I am making out that I see something. I'm just kidding myself, because, there isn't anything to see and I couldn't see much if there were.

I had just gotten the thing adjusted so that I could see some light through it, when the Boche decided that the three French aeroplanes overhead were getting too bold. They pumped up lead, lots of it. The planes wheeled and twisted back to safety. About thirty seconds later it began to rain lead. A flat iron or horse

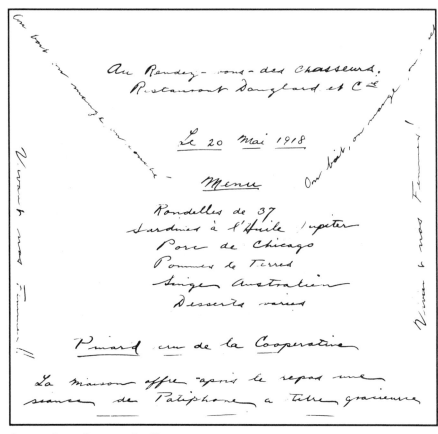

A menu for a dinner at the Chasseur.

Original sketch of Chasseur by Ernest H. Hinrichs, Sr.

shoe or something came down with a noise like a skyrocket not fifty feet from me. I lost interest in the periscope.

Treubel had walked on ahead, and I saw him stop before a dugout and stand staring through the doorway. I came up and peered over his shoulder down a flight of stairs. On the earthen floor lay two men in cowhide boots and dirty grey green uniforms. The face of the nearest was uncovered. Dull eyes stared up at us out of deep sockets. German dead; the first human wreckage of the war that I have seen. I turned away but Treubel did not move. He continued to stare fixedly at the face on the floor. It was an elderly face, with haggard features and unkempt grey mustache.

Why did not Treubel come on? I put my hand on his shoulder and said, "What's the idea of letting that Boche hypnotize you? Let's go."

He shook himself free. "Go on. Mind your own business!" he snarled.

I was so taken aback by this sudden turn of his unsociable nature, that the strangeness of the incident never occurred to me. Ten yards off I looked back and there was Treubel still motionless, apparently entirely unconscious of his surroundings, fascinated by the fixed eyes of the dead German.

He arrived at the Chasseur five minutes after I did and has hardly spoken a word since. This morning he volunteered to do extra time at the apparatus while Pompie, D'Anglard and I fixed up a place to eat on the terrace outside the dugout. It is getting warm and this is to be our summer dining room. The French were in a festive mood and invited two men from their cooperative canteen for dinner. We have just had a grand feast with much merriment and considerable wine.

D'Anglard made up a menu for the occasion. I am sorry that I could not get the original, but I have made a copy on the back of this sheet. When we thought we were finished, they brought out a bottle of champagne.

It is now five o'clock but the sun is still high in the sky. Its rays would be striking me full in the face were it not for the corrugated iron sun shade rigged up overhead and screened from inquisitive enemy airmen by many green bows.

I look to my left. About fifty feet away, seated at a table under a sunshade very much like this one, are ten American soldiers doing justice to a good supper. Beyond, at a slightly higher level, is a very creditable rustic summer house. When I look to my right I see another such picnic table this time on the terrace and shaded by a pine tree.

Rat—tat—tat—tat—tat—tat—that confounded machine gun is enough to wake the dead. Not a hundred feet away the little French gunner sits on a stump with the gun on a tripod before him. Every few minutes he pulls the trigger apparently to make sure that the apparatus is still in good working order. It is indirect fire; the muzzle of the gun is pointed over the hill. There are other noises to disturb my composition. Since I started writing, the air has been continually vibrating with the roar of distant aeroplane motors. Now they are much closer; I can distinguish two allied planes by the sound, and possibly three. "Wang! Crump!—Wang! Crump!—There go the Boche "Antis." The planes are too low to venture over the enemy lines; I can hear now that they have turned about. They will be back again in a minute. It is all in the day's work for them for three or four hours daily.

May 29th.

Yesterday evening, shortly after I had written the above, the Germans opened up an intense bombardment of our lines. This is the first time the enemy has really let loose his artillery since I came to the front. They had been unusually quiet all day. Then about 5 P.M. everything let go all at once. At the same time two German planes appeared over our lines very low, less than a thousand feet up, circling and dodging the shrapnel. The French machine gun started off with a roar and the nearest Boche went head first in a tail spin for the ground. We all thought he was hit. Later, we found he straightened out just before he hit and returned to his own lines.

The bombardment kept up for two hours. Our artillery came back strong. Most of the shooting was to the north of us but shells fell all along the line. By 7 P.M. things began to quiet down and the five of us gathered around our instruments discussing what had happened. D'Anglard had the French headset on and I had ours. The wires were unusually quiet.

"Perhaps the lines are broken so badly that we get nothing," D'Anglard suggested as he switched over to another line. "But they seldom go all to pieces. We got nothing unusual today. Treubel was on all morning. Where is his report? I should not have left it to him."

"What does this bombardment mean?" I asked, in my ignorance. "What do they gain by it? They don't seem to follow it up."

"If it is a local bombardment, it may not mean very much," said D'Anglard, becoming very serious. "It may be only nervousness, but I do not think so. The Boche is pushing things. It may be the beginning of another drive. They bombard all along the line to hide where they will strike and to keep us busy. Psst!"

He held up his hand. Something was coming over the wire. A rattling buzz, the click of a receiver and then clearly enough:

"Hello, hello—Caton!"

"Yes," came back, more distinct.

"How's everything?"

"There will be one load anyway and probably another before morning—got six men ready now. Road is safe. No gas!"

"Be right up."

The click of the receiver replaced and then silence.

Presently at seven o'clock the usual generator buzz began. The Boche were turning on their electric lights exactly on time. The generator noise is distracting but it does not make it impossible to hear other things. At exactly 7:15 P.M., a long enemy T.P.S.* came through fairly clear. Both D'Anglard and I took it down and then compared notes, correcting reports accordingly. It was in code, of course, but certainly not routine. D'Anglard considered it of such importance that he took it immediately to batallion headquarters to relay it back to Division Intelligence.

Pompie took D'Anglard's place beside me. The French were not trusting the instruments to us now. But the lines were silent, and presently I asked Pompie what he thought had happened or was happening. He felt my uneasines and immediately his boyish face relaxed.

"Nothing to worry about," he assured me. "This bombarding here is nothing. Up beyond Verdun or even further north it may mean something more serious. We hope to get the wireless communiques tonight. They may be interesting." He looked at his watch. "Nauen usually comes on at nine o'clock (ten in Germany). Perhaps Berlin will have something to tell."

At three minutes past nine by my watch, the rasping call of the great German wireless station came to us. Presently the operator launched into the official report. These wireless operators send too fast for me and try as I would, with my little training I could not keep up with him. Pompie was laboring hard to get it but leaving out a word now and again to keep up.

"Hey! Treubel!" I called, "come here and take this enemy press for us, will you?" Treubel appeared in the doorway and with a yawn took my headset and immediately began to write the involved German sentences of the report. I read over his shoulder:

Berlin, May 28,
Official Report. (translated)

On the Kemmel and Lys battlefields and on both sides of the Somme and Avre the artillery duels increased in intensity yesterday morning. Between Vooremezeele and Locre we penetrated the French lines and brought back more than 300 prisoners.

The attack of the German Crown Prince to the south of Laon led to complete success. We completely defeated the French and English divisions stationed there.

The Army of General Von Boehm took Chemin des Dames by storm. The long ridge against which the great attempt of the French to break through collapsed in the spring of 1917 and which we evacuated in the autumn of last year is again in our hands.

---

* Note: (Author's Handwriting) T.P.S. = Telegraph par soile = ground telegraph.

After tremendous artillery preparation, our infantry at daybreak found its way across the Ailettes river between Vauxaillon and Craonne, and penetrated the English lines further east between Corbeny and the Aisne. Completely taken by surprise, the occupants of the first enemy line generally offered only slight resistance.

In the early hours of the morning Pinon, Chavigon, Fort Malmaison, Courtecon, Cerney, the Winterberg and Craonne the Villerberg and fortified works near and to the north of Berry au Bac were taken by storm.

Toward afternoon we reached the Aisne between Vailly and Barray au Bac. Vailley was taken. The crater field of last year's spring and autumn fighting was thus captured in uninterrupted attacking pressure.

In the afternoon the attack continued. Between Vauxaillon and Vailly we are in the heights near Newville and Loffaux and north of Conde.

Between Barry au Bac and Brimont we crossed the Aisne and carried the battle line into an area that had remained untouched by the war since 1914. The enemy was driven from the fortified wooded heights on the southern bank of the river. Between Vailly and Beaurieux we reached the heights due north of the Vesele river.

The army of General Von Buelow threw the enemy out of strong positions between Sapiegneul and Brimont back across the Aisne-Marne canal and took by storm Cormicy, Cauroy and Loivre.

Up to the present 15,000 prisoners are reported.

Between the Meuse and the Moselle, on the Lorraine front, the fighting activity revived. Advances into the enemy lines resulted in the bringing in of more than 150 prisoners belonging to French and American regiments.*

That ended the official report. Press followed, a steady stream of dots and dashes coming from the instruments for almost two hours. We did not bother to take it down; the report told enough and the press would only go into details. Treubel went back to bed. D'Anglard came in with the news from batallion headquarters that there were casualties up the line, but the damage here was nil.

We settled down to our vigil; we were to be on until two o'clock. At 1 A.M., a little before by my watch, the call of the Eiffel tower came in clear and sharp. FL—FL—FL —FL—FL—for a full minute this kept up and then the operator began rolling out the French Communique:

Paris, May 28, (translated)

Last night and today, the enemy, taking advantage of his numerical superiority, renewed his thrust more strongly toward the southwest of Soissons. ——

He got no further; a terrific detonation split the air and then explosions followed fast one after the other. The candle flickered from the earth tremors and the air concussions. D'Anglard drew in his breath with a long low whistle. Pushing back his chair, he strode across the room and opened the door leading out on the terrace. I followed on his heels.

---

*   Note: (Longhand by Author) This is the actual report of May 28th.

We stood in the doorway and stared into the belabored night. A clear starlit sky crackled and whined as though in torture. The distant guns roared but the heavy explosions nearby had ceased. Over the hill to the east and south, the vault of the heavens pulsated, and the earth under our feet quivered intermittently, as though the universe were about to be shaken apart. As we stood in the doorway, the sky to the west lit up in four or five places and a few seconds later came the heavy boom of our own batteries answering the enemy fire. Over our heads the shells screeched in both directions but none fell nearby.

"Gas," said D'Anglard, "but most of it is falling over there." He nodded to the north and sniffed the air cautiously. The others were aroused by this time and we brought our masks to the alert position.

"Village Nègre is getting it thick," D'Anglard explained. "The valley soon will be full of gas. It will be very unhealthy before morning. This is a good position. They won't bother us here; the valley is easier."

We all lit pipes or cigarettes; the cognac bottle appeared and was passed around. By two o'clock the bombardment was becoming monotonous. I was very sleepy and had lost interest, whether from lack of sleep or the effect of the cognac. D'Anglard and I turned in with the precaution of leaving our shoes on. I was asleep immediately and slept until 7 A.M. when Papa Dubois called me for breakfast. The chill of the morning air was penetrating as I went out on the terrace. The first rays of the sun were striking the top of the hill. A mist hung in the valley. The distant hum of an aeroplane motor was the only sound of the war.

At eight o'clock our relief had not arrived, so Treubel and I started back. Halfway down the slope we met Israel and Beaman, who were to take our places, laboring slowly up the hill with gas masks on. Seeing us they removed masks and took deep breaths of clean morning air.

"Valley is full of gas," Beaman puffed, mopping his face. "Battalion above Village Nègre is pretty near wiped out. They're rushing them back to the hospital as fast as they can, but not fast enough. You can't expect wounded men to live in air like that."

Despite this warning, Treubel and I proceeded jauntily down the trail. Totally inexperienced with gas,[2] we pretended that we were wise. Some two hundred yards from the Red Cross station a peculiar taint was in the air, but certainly that was harmless. There were many fresh shell holes and the smell was of the rotten earth.

"Hey there!" a voice called from across the valley. We looked up to see a man gesticulating wildly, waving us back. "Gaa-ss! You da—— foo——!" The first word was clear enough. We put our masks on in a hurry. Ignorance is a dangerous companion.

The valley had received a severe beating. The fresh spring foliage was withered and yellow; pock marks studded the fields. The Red Cross station was full of men. An ambulance came up as we approached. Two men with masks on, working in silence, lifted blanketed forms on stretchers into the back. I've learned since that the two companies holding that front were nearly annihilated. Over 300 men are in the hospital at Baccarat.

May 30th.

Today, Decoration day, we had the memorial services for the men recently killed. It was a very impressive ceremony held in the little graveyard outside of Pexonne. The Colonel of the 168th and the Brigadier General spoke. The graves were decorated with flowers by the village children and saluted by officers. The regimental band played the Star-Spangled Banner, then three volleys were fired over the graves, and after prayer by the chaplain, "taps" were sounded.[3]

June 1st.

Last night the wireless reports were most interesting. The way the French reacted you'd think the Germans were in Paris. I copied off the important parts.

Berlin, May 31st.

On the front from Noyon to the west of Rheims our attack is progressing favorably. ———

The rear positions of the enemy at Arcy and Grand Rozoy were pierced. To the south of Fère-en-Tardenois we reached the Marne. The heights of Sainte Gemme, Romigny, and Château Thierry are in our possession. ———

The number of prisoners and booty are increasing continuously. More than 45,000 prisoners, including one French and one English General, and more than 400 guns and thousands of machine guns have been taken.

This report threw the French into dismay. They could not believe it. D'Anglard kept repeating "Thierry—the Marne—it is too far—the Americans are too late."

"Where are these places?" I asked. "Have they broken through?"

"Advanced over thirty miles in a few days—that looks like it." He began scolding me as though I could help it. "Bombarding Paris—at its gates—Americans, Bah! You know nothing—you take too long."[4]

With that he turned from me and taking up the report went into the back room, where I heard the three "Frogs" in earnest conversation until late.

Then, when we got this French report they were speechless:

Paris. (translated)

The troops covering Reims have withdrawn behind the Aine canal, northwest of the town.

The battle took on particular violence on our left wing. In the region of Soissons, after stubborn resistance and fighting in the streets, our troops evacuated the town ———

I have been doing a lot of thinking here lately and have called myself an ass a good many times. Woefully incompetent, an abject dreamer suddenly awakened to reality. It is very evident that this war is still not running exactly as the Allies would like it to go. To win this war will be a long hard job and, before it is over, we will all get our fill of it. I am taking a much greater interest in my Colt. Peterson got hold of a bag of pistol ammunition somewhere and this morning we went over to a stone quarry for a little target practice. My God! I couldn't hit a barn door. After some twenty shots I had a little better control, the gun at least didn't act like it was going to jump out of my hand when it went off. I still blink at each shot, and if I ever get into a tight place, I know I'll hurl the damn automatic at the enemy. I've never thrown a hand grenade, and right now every time I come into contact with one of those iron pears I handle it as a small boy does his first giant cracker. I'm scared of it but I want to make it go off. Just outside of Langres when we were at the signal school, I watched three French-men stage a grenade raid demonstration for a group of American officers. They crept on their stomachs toward an imagined enemy outpost. At a signal they threw their grenades and then closed in with bayoneted rifles. They did it so easily.

June 2nd.

It's 9:30 P.M. I'm at the apparatus. It has been an interesting day. We caught some enemy talk today; the first real message at the Chasseur. The men at the Dragoon say that they have gotten quite a little. While we were at lunch, Treubel took down an enemy telephone conversation that astounded the French. Pompie and Le Maire had been out all morning patching the lines. We were eating when Treubel came out with a scribbled piece of paper. D'Anglard looked at it and rose in his seat.

"What's this? Treubel, did you hear this?" he asked incredulously.

Treubel insisted that he had.

"When?" asked D'Anglard.

"Just now, not ten minutes ago," said Treubel.

D'Anglard read it for the benefit of us all. I cannot remember the exact words, but it was something like this:

Hallo! Hallo! Katzenkus?—Maller ist es—Für Leutnant Willmann, ist er da?—
Wer, ruft?—
Major Pfaltz will selbst sprechen.
Ein moment—
Hallo—Leutnant Willmann zu Befehl!
Wie viele Gaskugeln haben sie noch?—
900–77 und nicht mehr wie 80–150.—
Ich schicke ihnen aus Kristkogal 3000 mehr 77 und 300–150.—
Jetzt?—
Sofort. (Click)—(Click)
Hallo! Hallo! Herr Major Pfaltz!—
Malar spricht.
Ist er schon weg? Verdammt. (click)[5]

We listened, two on, all afternoon and there was no more talk, only routine calls.

That message we sent right into headquarters and we have been wondering all evening how they liked it. Treubel still insists he heard it and the French seem to believe him.

All afternoon our observation planes have been very busy and this evening Allied long-range guns have been doing most of the shooting.

June 4th.

Treubel is gone. He came out with another message when the Frenchman beside him removed his headset for a few minutes. It was more elaborate than the first. That precipitated a row, almost a war, at the Chasseur. He swore he heard it, and we all doubted him but could prove nothing. The little son-of-a-gun began to get nasty. D'Anglard said it was imagination, hallucination, and that men often do queer tricks at the front. That is a most charitable explanation.

Anyway, Lieutenant Thompson arrived yesterday with a division intelligence officer. Treubel got the third degree, but they could prove nothing. They took him out of this work because they could not trust him. It happened that "Kristkogal" and "Katzenkus" were known places in the German lines. Did he hear them at another station? Was it imagination or deliberate forgery? Damned if I know, but I am glad he is off my hands. I hope I never see him again.

The Lieutenant brought much mail. Five letters for me; the first for two weeks. Nothing like news from home to set the world right again. I needed them badly after this Treubel affair.*

June 7th.

Ever since the first attack of May 28th, when the raid on the Village Nègre section took place, this front has been more active. The enemy started that day his big effort to get through the lines up north, and the wireless reports do not sound good at all. Here the Boche has been much freer with his ammunition; gas has been sent over frequently. We now sleep in Pexonne with our masks close beside us. We have been disturbed three times in the early hours by gas alarms.

The other day after supper I strolled up town, that is, to the village square, and bought a Franc's worth of walnuts. The sun had just sunk below the horizon; the clouds were still tinged with the afterglow. There was not a sound of war in the air. The artillery was taking a day off. It was Sunday. Munching walnuts, I wandered down the road. Presently, the great silvery moon rose from behind a bank of clouds. It was full. It was hard to realize that the war was still going on.

I was filled with the futility of life. The beauty of the evening, instead of inspiring me, depressed me. What a mess man has made of existence. What business have I to be here anyway? Homesickness seized me. I'm no soldier and I cannot seem to work up any personal hatred of the Germans. The great adventure of coming overseas had suddenly begun to pall. I began to wish I had said "no" when they asked me if I were willing to go. They gave us that opportunity at Camp Vaile when we were put on the overseas list. But we never hesitated in our reply. It was the great adventure and we knew that the alternative in the States would not be pleasant. Always in the back of my mind had been the idea that the war was drawing to a close and that we would not see much active service because the Germans were about starved, and the odds against them were so great that they would have to quit or be completely wiped out. Now, for three months they have been pushing steadily forward and the French become more serious daily, and I am not even suited for the small task that has been assigned to me.

I returned slowly to quarters and turned in early after writing a letter home, the sending of which I have since regretted. The night was still calm and silent so that in less than five minutes I was sound asleep.

Almost immediately, so it seemed, I was jolted back to consciousness. Hell had broken loose. Explosions followed each other thick and fast. The air was pulsing with the shocks and the room was constantly illuminated as by lightning flashes. Then a little piece of shrapnel came tearing through the linen which had long ago replaced the glass on the window frame. I looked at my luminous Ingersoll—3:10 A.M.

---

* Author's Note: (Added in longhand at a later date)
The Treubel episode is cut rather short. More could be made of it. Treubel had been mixed up in the Telefunken[6] wireless affair in the States and had been released because he was considered only an employee. He had immediately enlisted in the Villa expedition to the Mexican border and because of good service and apparent anti-German attitude had gained confidence. His object in faking, of course, would be to hold the 42nd Division on this front when it was much needed elsewhere. He may have partially succeeded.

As I look back on the affair now, I do not believe that Treubel was consciously disloyal when he came overseas. He was too frank in telling us his past history. But I believe that continual reception of the German press reports and the sight of the German dead suddenly made him realize what the war was all about.

"Time to beat it for the cellar," I yelled.

Keller across the room was already slipping into his shoes and swearing away at the damn sons of bitches for waking him up at such an ungodly hour. In the hall we could hear the Frenchmen come tumbling down the steps, yelling at the top of their lungs. Probably wanted to make sure we were all awake.

"Grab your overcoat and gas mask and come on," bawled Keller, as a couple of extra violent detonations made the floor shake. I did not have to be told twice, the air concussions were all the urging I needed. I only stopped for my flashlight and a can of Velvet.[7]

Even as we were running down the hall the bombardment changed. There were just as many shells coming over but only about half of them ended in real explosions; the rest simply went "plop." We knew what that meant. The blanket was fastened over the entrance to the cellar, and everybody got out gas masks.

A weird company we were, six of us Americans and about fifteen French including a woman and her ten year old son from the house next door. Some house owners still remain in Pexonne. They cling desperately to their homes as the only hope of preventing the utter ruin of their property and because there is no place to go. Until two weeks ago, Pexonne had been comparatively immune to shellfire for more than a year. The French say that there was a tacit agreement between the opponents. "If you don't shell my town I won't shell yours." It was a "bon secteur" indeed, but now the French say "bon secteur!" ironically every time the row starts.

Everybody immediately began to smoke—for this I had brought the Velvet. It is claimed that the smoker is less affected by gas. Two fellows came in a little later. They had their masks on and said the stuff was already thick outside. In entering they had lifted the blanket and a little gas got in. Within ten seconds we were transformed into a group of goblins, with huge round eyes and most extraordinary snoots. The two candles flickered dimly. Through our masks we could not smoke, and all talk was muffled into incoherent goblin grumblings. Our shadows danced wildly on the whitewashed walls and low arched ceiling. The space was narrow and already misty with tobacco smoke.

For half an hour we stood eyeing each other and listening to the racket outside. Then some brave spirit stuck his finger under the side of his mask and took a sniff. He cocked his head on one side like a chef sampling soup, then stuck two fingers under his mask and took two sniffs. Finally convinced, he tore off his snoot and announced that the air was pure. Immediately the goblins were changed into a company of human beings. Everybody was asking for cigarettes or tobacco. Jokes went the rounds; all talked at once.

Outside there were fewer big explosions and more of the dull sickly thuds which mean gas. This kept up until about 4:50; then things began to quiet down. Two warwise Frenchmen sniffed at the curtain, put masks on and ventured up into the hall. We followed. It was getting light. A breeze had sprung up and the gas was quickly being blown away. A few minutes later we removed our masks.

But now a new rumpus started—the "Wang! Crump!" of the "Archies"* and the rattle of machine guns punctuated the roar of an aeroplane close overhead. We crowded to the front and rear doors and peered out. A Boche plane was circling and swooping over the town not five hundred feet up. We saw him dive and cut loose with his machine gun at the street. Then he must have seen us for he made a quarter turn

---

* Note: (Author's Handwriting) Anti-aircraft Batteries.

and came straight at us. I stayed just long enough to see the fire spurt from his machine guns a couple of times, then ducked. He roared not fifty feet over the house. We crowded to the front door to see him sail away toward his own lines.

Occasional gas shells were still falling and the air was far from pure. The gas had an odd smell. There was something familiar about it, but I cannot place it. It was somewhat like garlic, but rottener. Once before they shot over some gas that smelled much like new mown hay. It did not seem dangerous at all. I think this was mustard gas; it produced huge water blisters and affected the eyes.

The Boche had gone and the bombardment had finally stopped. Two French aeroplanes were patrolling the sky, sweeping back and forth along the line. We went out to see what damage had been done. The landscape was but little changed. The pottery factory had again received most attention. Our potato patch was badly messed up and the road looked like a telescopic picture of the moon. Little sinking holes made by gas shells were everywhere. There was a big crater some twelve feet across less than fifty feet from our house. This shell had thrown dirt all over the place. A piece of metal had gone clear through a telephone pole, and the wires were scattered all around. Another high explosive struck the rear of the house across the way, where American troops were quartered, They were in the cellar, and only two were injured.

Chapter 3

The Rainbow Moves Out

After America's entry into World War I, then Major Douglas MacArthur suggested to Secretary Of War Newton Baker the creation of a division that drew its component outfits from as many areas of the Union as possible. The Division chosen for this was the 42nd and, because of its composition, it received the nickname of Rainbow. This was done in an attempt to unify the country behind the idea of participation in an overseas war. The Division Headquarters arrived in France on November 1, 1917. After landing, the troops were trained further and put in the line in the same area as my father. Since these component units had had previous training, it was possible to get American troops into action in France earlier than would otherwise have been the case. Subsequent units that arrived later in France were composed of more draftees and other types of replacements. The contrast between better trained soldiers and new arrivals is very evident. It was only a little over a month after being withdrawn from the "bon Secteur" that the Rainbow Division was involved in violent action at the Ourcq river.[1]

June 22nd.

The 42nd Division is moving out of here* and the 77th, a New York Draft Division, is moving into the line. These men don't look so good. They are green as grass and lack the spirit of the 42nd. The Boche, of course, let them have the works immediately and it was some baptism they got.

One enemy battery is raising the devil in Pexonne these days. This is no longer the sleepy little village it used to be. Most of the civilians have moved out and I am told the rest will be ordered out soon. A high explosive struck our village church squarely yesterday and knocked a hole in it about twenty feet in diameter. This church had stood practically unharmed through four years of war, and now it caves in.

---

* Note: (Typed by Author) This is three weeks after the Treubel Episode.

Regimental H. Q. has been moved to Neufmaison, a village two miles further back, and Pexonne has very few troops in it now. We have had trouble getting rations. Yesterday, Keller and I were reading in the "Non-Coms Club." In walked a doughboy. "The Lieutenant Colonel is outside," he said. "Wants to speak to one of the fellows in the P.T.B. service."

We looked at each other. What the devil could he want? A nuisance to have to put on shoes and adjust leggings and button jackets just to be looked at. We followed the soldier out. The officer was standing by his car and a Lieutenant with a notebook stood beside him.

"You men in the listening service?" the big man asked.

"Yes sir." We saluted.

"How do you get your meals?" was his next question.

We explained our difficulties. The signal platoon had refused us rations. The other kitchen in town was continually changing and at each change we had difficulty explaining why we wanted two days' rations and what we were doing around town anyway. They couldn't understand why we didn't eat with our outfit, and looked suspicious when we described the nature of our outfit. The root of the matter was that we wanted to eat at the signal platoon kitchen because the food was better.

After more questions and answers, the colonel turned to the lieutenant and said: "Tell Lieutenant Woods of the signal platoon that these men will eat with the signal platoon by order of the commanding general."

The Lieutenant scribbled in his note book.

"If you have any more trouble," continued the Colonel, addressing us, "call up James and ask for the division intelligence officer." He stepped into his car and drove off.

The former grouchy mess sergeant, who had refused us eats, was a changed man when we came up for supper.

"You're here to stay this time," he smiled pleasantly. Then he turned to his cook.

"Give them all they want," he ordered. "Heap it on."

The sergeant kept eyeing us as we were eating. Presently he came forward.

"Come again if you want some more. Who the hell are you fellows, anyhow?" he queried. "Got lieutenant colonels and commanding generals to see that twelve men get enough to eat, and eat at this kitchen and not the one down the street."

"Well you see," explained Keller, "when we get those two days' rations we go over into the German lines and ask the Heinies what they are going to do next and tell the General all about it. Naturally he appreciated it and thinks we are due a good feed."

"Oh! Yeah!" said the mess sergeant.

In this connection the following letter is of interest:

G. H. Q. - A. E. F.

Office of the Chief Signal Officer.   10th May 1918
From: Officer in charge, Radio Division, O.C.S.O. - A.E.F.
To: Captain Robert Loghry, Radio Officer, G. H. Q. - A.E.F.
Subject: Letter of commendation from Chief Signal Officer.

1. The Chief Signal Officer has forwarded the following letter, dated May 7th, Communicating his appreciation of the good work being done by the officers and men of the Radio Division.

The Chief Signal Officer directs me to advise you that he has received under secret cover, from A.C. of S.G. at G.H.Q., a most commendatory report on the operations of the Radio Division of the Signal Corps. For obvious reasons specific dates and data obtained from the intercept stations cannot be given. The following extract from the report, however, is furnished for your information.

The net result has been that in the period of ——— days the information furnished by the Radio Intelligence Section has probably saved more men than are engaged in the service. Such results would have been impossible without the energetic and loyal cooperation of the Signal Corps. Officers and men of the Radio Intelligence deserve the highest commendation.

The Chief Signal Officer also desires me to express his own appreciation of the splendid work being done by the officers and men of your division.

(Sd) Sosthenes Behn
Major S.R.L. Execution Officer

Now, isn't that sweet. What are they trying to do—kid us along? Will somebody please tell me what all those letters mean? And this is the first time I have ever heard of an Execution Officer in this Army.

I had a bath the other day, the first real one since I have been on the line. The village horse trough is now the community bath tub. It is big enough to hold two or three men lined up. Boy, was that water cold.

June 24th.

Just returned from Chasseur. These new line troops are a nuisance. They are skittish and sticklers for form. We had to show our passes and repeat the counter-sign as we went by sentries. The outpost arrested D'Anglard and Pompie yesterday as suspicious characters. It was a good joke on them but not so pleasant at the time.

They had gone out in the morning to repair the line which had been smashed by shell fire during the night. The new U.S. troops have taken over the outpost positions formerly occupied by the French. The advance squad reluctantly allowed the French-men to pass. They negotiated the entanglement with a skill won by two years of practice. Out of sight of every living soul, in the dreariest and most unhealthy place on earth, they worked for two hours. They completed the job and bethought them of dinner. Very tired and very dirty, they started back through the "barbele."

Suddenly—"Halt!"

The forward Frenchman got his eyes above the mud line and found himself staring into the muzzle of an Enfield. The face behind the rifle did not look at all pleasant. Two more men appeared and the three seemed to be arguing. Finally they motioned the Frenchmen to come on, all the while keeping him covered with the rifle.

D'Anglard squirmed through the entanglement. Immediately his hands were tied and his pistol taken from him. Pompie submitted meekly to the same treatment. They tried to explain who they were and what they were doing, but it was no use.

No, the corporal of that outpost was certain that they were spies. They had gone over to communicate with the enemy. What earthly business could keep two men in No-Man's-Land in broad daylight for two hours? No one goes into No-Man's-Land in the daytime. On both sides, sentinels are ever on the alert for moving objects; it would be necessary to "keep your head down" all the time.

"Working on wires?" repeated the corporal doubtfully. "That won't do. The signal Corps does some da—— fool stunts but it doesn't send two Frenchmen to string phone leads in No-Man's-Land. Soon you will be telling us you were putting a pole line out there. You can tell the major all about it; I ain't got time to listen. Forward, March!"

I was setting the table for dinner under the camouflaged screening before the Chasseur dugout. I had laid out six plates and placed a steaming soup tureen in the middle of the table with the Pinard (vin Rouge) bottles artistically on either side: I was surveying my work critically. I caught a whiff now and then of frying country sausage under the skillful touch of Lavasieur.

Suddenly two bedraggled poilus came around the corner followed by a very serious U.S. soldier with fixed bayonet. The prisoners fairly howled with laughter when they saw me. Their predicament seemed to tickle them immensely. When the guard saw that I knew them he looked a little sheepish, but stuck to his purpose, urging them on toward Battalion Headquarters.

There was an investigation. The men were identified and arrangements made for passes to be issued whenever we want to go into No-Man's-Land. The French can't get over that. It is a new one on them, and they keep joking about it. These new troops are so recently from the States that they see spies everywhere. A few days ago a squad was sent to search the old pottery factory because somebody claimed he saw a blinking light in a dormer window. Keller says two Frenchmen at the Dragon were arrested the day before yesterday. They were overheard talking German in the dugout and were sent all the way to Baccarat and given a regular third degree. The French Adjutant had to go to Baccarat in the morning to identify them; nobody else would do.

July 4th.

Ten days have passed since my last writing and much has happened. On the morning of the 28th of June when Beaman and I arrived at the Chasseur for our turn of duty, we found the whole sector deserted. The men of our service were the only people left within a half mile. The infantry detachments had received orders to retire at four in the afternoon of the previous day and had all withdrawn during the night. We had received no instructions and so had to stay. We tried the telephone. It was dead. We went over to the former battalion headquarters dugout and found everything in the greatest confusion. The evacuation had evidently been hurried. The telephone switchboard was torn out. Junk was scattered all around; there were gas masks, shoes, books, tins of emergency rations, hundreds of clips of rifle ammunition, but the one thing we wanted, Colt .45 ammunition, we could not find. What did it all mean? Was there anyone in the front line? Or was the Boche free to come over if he chose?

D'Anglard set out to the rear to get information and orders. The uneasiness of the French was most apparent and, of course, most contagious. Here were the five of us left in this isolated position. I looked around at the empty dugouts which had been teeming with infantry men. All were deserted. I determined to see for myself what there was between us and the Boche.

Leaving Pompie and Beaman at the apparatus I went alone over the hill. This section had received a copious shelling and considerable gas about a week previously. The woods were badly smashed up and I had to jump over splintered tree trunks and detour broken branches all the way. The leaves were still on but yellow and shriveled. Even much of the foliage still standing was bleached and dried by the gas.

In the middle of the woods there was a heavy entanglement and a group of big dugouts. It was the line position formerly occupied by an infantry company. I searched the dugouts. There were several cases of grenades, thousands of rounds of rifle ammunition, several "musettes" of automatic rifle shells and five or six sealed and crated tins of reserve rations. There was not a human being in sight.

I went on. At the junction of the Boyau Real and the Boyau Malgrave I hesitated, undecided which trench to take. I listened. The front line was less than a hundred yards from here and yet there was no sound. I drew my automatic and pulled the slide back. For some reason I chose the trench Malgrave.

"If there are sentries," I thought, "there will be a post at the end of this."

I trudged on, making as little noise as possible, stooping frequently under camouflaging and turning corners cautiously. I passed two or three cross trenches. The down grade became steeper, the twists and turns and camouflage more numerous. The trees on the hillside were all shot to pieces. The ground was very rough and full of shell craters. I came to the dugout trench. At the head of the steps leading down I stopped with drawn pistol.

Here was confusion worse confounded; ration tins, grenades, trench tools, flares, wire, and all kinds of old equipment strewn around. As I peered into the black doorway, a huge rat scuttled across the threshold. Then I knew that the place was deserted. I called aloud anyway.

"Is anybody here?" No answer.

I came back to the communication trench. It ran on down the hill and was much exposed. A little farther on barbed wire blocked it. At this point the German first line is just on the other slope of the little valley not a hundred yards away.

I returned to Boyau Real and followed that out. In the cross trench at the end I finally found a few sleepy men. An American private was seated before a prismatic binocular rigged up on a graduated sector stand. He was surprised to see me and looked me up and down rather doubtfully as I approached.

"Well," I said cheerfully, "I'm glad there is somebody on watch in the line."

A Frenchman, who had been snoozing peacefully on a little hay in the bottom of the trench, raised himself on one elbow and began chewing on a piece of straw. Beyond him I saw two pairs of legs whose owners were sound asleep in recesses in the side of the ditch.

I had received no answer. These men appeared to resent my intrusion and to question my right to be there. I hastened to explain that I was from the radio listening station over the hill and had come up to find out if there was anybody in the line.

"Don't talk so loud," rebuked the observer in a low voice. "Do you want to see the corporal? He's asleep back there."

"No, you'll do," I assured him in a whisper. "Can you see anything through that glass?"

"Hope to tell you," the man grinned, all his resentment gone at my recognition of him and his work. I glued my eyes to the binoculars and was very much disappointed in the view. In the foreground there was nothing but trees and dense foliage. Beyond, through a gap in the forest, the open country was visible, but hazy with no definitely distinguishable landmarks.

"Can't see a thing," I admitted. "What are you supposed to look at?"

"Don't change the position of the glass or the focus," he cautioned, as I began to fiddle with the binoculars. "It's set just right," he continued, taking another peep to make sure. "Just above the leaves is a road and a telephone line. Most of the road is camouflaged but from here you can see anything going by. A wagon passed just before you came. Take another look. See the road just over the green? Now a little higher up and to the left is the village. Rather badly smashed but a village none the less, and beyond that a white line of road leading back between rows of trees."

"Right you are," I agreed. "I didn't see anything the first time I looked but now you point it out, it's a road all right and if there were any troop movements you'd see them. But what is that tower away off there on the horizon?"

"Don't know," he said, "It's way back five miles or more near a town. All we do is watch the roads."

I stayed and talked with the observer quite a while. They came on duty the evening before and were to be relieved at dusk. Had been very alert all night and were sleeping all day. They had orders to shoot up a rocket at the first sign of a German advance and then to retire.

"Very encouraging for us." I thought. "Evidently a raid or push is expected."

I returned to the Chasseur through the uncannily silent woods, without seeing a soul. D'Anglard had returned from "Three Pines," the new battalion headquarters, which was more than a half mile to the rear. The major knew nothing. Orders to withdraw had come the day before and they had moved during the night. D'Anglard had telephoned Division Intelligence for orders and had been told to stay where we were.

The three Frenchmen were in earnest and excited conversation, speaking rapidly in French. It was evident that they didn't like the turn of events.

"Do you think there is much danger here? Will the Germans come over?" I quizzed innocently. I had never seen D'Anglard so excited before.

"Ha!" he exclaimed. "They certainly will come over. When they find that there is no one in the line, their patrols will penetrate deeper and deeper. There will not be so much danger tonight, but tomorrow night or the next night. But that is the least of it. If the Germans start an offensive, the French will place their artillery barrage on this hill. Right here they will shoot. Here! Here!" The man screwed up his face as though he had eaten a sour pickle and paced up and down stamping and waving his arms.

"But surely we won't have to stay here; if the row starts we will go back."

"Go back! Ha! Ha! Ha! Ha!" D'Anglard laughed rather insanely, I thought. Presently he stopped right before me, calmed down a bit, and continued in an even expressionless voice. "Hinrichs, I don't want to alarm you too much, but you don't know this war. We five men mean nothing to those in command. They need us here for the information that our apparatus may give. If something starts, our work is done, and we cease to exist so far as the command is concerned. A hurricane of shells will be dropped here. We will have to leave in the midst and withdraw across the valley to "Three Pines." If we escape the explosions on the hill, the gas in the valley will get us. We would do better to stay in the dugout and trust to luck, although the Chasseur is not made to be shot at from the French side."

D'Anglard's speech sobered us all for a while, but once we had resigned ourselves to our new isolation, the excellent dinner prepared by Lavasieur and the warm summer sun raised our spirits to the bubbling point.

I was at the instruments in the afternoon and those two kids, Hogel and Beaman, roamed all over the neighborhood collecting treasures out of abandoned dugouts.

They brought to our cave upholstered chairs, beautiful gilt mirrors, wash basins of china, abandoned rifles and a handsome clock. There were considerable eats including canned salmon and roast beef, sugar, coffee, and mineral water. By evening the Chasseur was a palace. But the greatest treasure of all they discovered in a company P.C. almost a half mile to the south, several hundred rounds of .45 ammunition.

After supper, while it was still light, we had target practice before the dugout and then began throwing grenades down the hill for the experience and love of the racket, until the French made us stop for fear the infantry would think the Germans were over.

About ten in the evening French 155's started shooting into the German lines. We could see the flash of the guns, then a few seconds later, the dull boom of the discharge, and at the same time the hair raising shriek of the shell close overhead followed almost immediately by the heavy explosion.

The Germans did not return the fire. I went to bed about eleven after reading the official report from Berlin.

I could not get to sleep, not because of the report or the whine of the shells overhead, but because of the fuss the rats were making. They were swarming to us from all over the sector, and kept scampering around the place and running over my bunk until I was afraid to put so much as my nose out for fear of getting it bitten off.

Dawn broke bright and clear. I came out on the terrace to relieve myself as the red disc of the sun gleamed through the tree trunks just over the hill. Deadly silence reigned except for the hum of the morning air patrol high overhead. The station receipts for the night were very scanty. I almost suspected the boys had slept on duty. There were a few routine enemy calls and the recorded start and stop of the generator.

Most of that day we waged war on the rats. It was a relentless war, exciting and diverting. Here at least one saw the enemy once in a while and got into personal encounter. A huge rodent had scuttered across the bunk room and darted into a hole against the rear wall. We put scraps of corn-willy (canned corn beef) near the opening and Pompie sat patiently on a stool with bayoneted rifle, motionless, waiting for Mr. Rat to come out. There was a wager between the Frenchmen that Pompie could not kill the rat with the bayonet. We had already killed four with rifles, shovels, and picks.

Very patiently we waited. Again and again a whiskered snoot and shiny eyes appeared in the opening, only to be withdrawn. Finally the bayonet flashed, there was a squeal and Pompie had him pinned by the hind quarter. He performed a dance of triumph with the rat dangling on the bayonet and then we held a mock funeral service. Five neat little graves in a row, a volley of revolver shots over the graves and taps on Pompie's tin fife.

In the afternoon more victims were added to the cemetery.

After dark wagons came and hauled away piles of *minenwerfers* and other ammunition left on the road. It was the first human activity we had seen in two days.

For two more days we stayed in isolation and then on the evening of July second came Malard with the P. T. B. move wagon. We dismantled the apparatus, placed on the cart the amplifiers and accumulators, etc., together with such personal treasures as we could pile on, and said good-bye to Chasseur forever.

Chapter 4

The Deserted Village

While this book is in the main faithfully taken from notes made at the time of occurrence, this extremely short chapter is an exception. There is a penciled note on the bottom of the manuscript in my father's handwriting to the effect that this gloomy description of the village of Badonvillers has been taken from a letter written home to one of his brothers. The letter was undoubtedly returned to him after the war.

Five men, three French and two American; a hand drawn cart which rumbles heavily with steel on stone over the hard faced road. Low hanging, lead hued clouds are hastening the gloom of fast approaching night. The plague, God's wrath, predestined desolation, what is it that holds this village in its grip?

The noise of steel shod wheels echoes on shattered walls, reverberates down dismal wreckage strewn side streets and roars against the town hall's battered facade. Surely the place is stricken with the pestilence. But no, look close, it is worse than the plague. The streets and buildings themselves have leprosy.

The time worn walls are pitted and freshly scarred. Shutters, carefully closed by departed occupants, hang on one hinge by cracked and splintered casements. Many roofs are missing, broken tiles litter the streets. Crumbling walls, mounds of masonry and charred beams a silent story tell; of human misery, of the end result of unleashed human hate.

The cart rolls on to lower ground; uneasily the men sniff the air. The peculiar musty odor of the place is only too familiar. They hurry on, swing a corner to the left and at a square beyond are halted by a sentry. A short parley, and the five pass out through a wire barricade into the country.

Night has swallowed them. Low overhead the gathering heavy clouds are releasing a fine misty drizzle. Tomorrow is the fourth of July.

Author's note on the reverse of this postcard reads:
I walked along here every two days for three months, often under shell fire. This is not over a half mile from front line. Badonviller is badly wrecked.

Author's caption was:
This looks different now. No civilians when we were here. I passed along this street every two days on the way to post and back.

Part II

Preface to Part II

History has shown that the first week of July 1918 was the turning point of the war. All through the spring, the Germans had exerted tremendous pressure against the Allied lines and the power of their repeated thrusts had produced a critical situation. For over a month a crisis among the Allies threatened and the issue hung in the balance. French morale had reached a low ebb. Thousands were fleeing from Paris and the government was preparing to move to Bordeaux.

Finally the incoming tide of American Divisions began to tell and the Germans lost the initiative, never to regain it.*

I submit these writings for what they are worth. Much must be omitted for the sake of brevity. Part II begins with the entire outlook of the war changed. German hopes gone and Allied morale at a high pitch. The Marne salient has been reduced and the American First Army is being formed.

---

* Note: It is interesting to note that, at this point in my father's original manuscript, which was absolutely as written above, that there is a very shakily written question mark followed by large shaky printing which says "Hitler? World War II." After his retirement from dentistry he took up the hobby of oil painting. One of his pictures showed three West German soldiers at present arms. He titled it "Soldiers of the third World War." Sometimes he would get out the manuscript and think back to fifty years earlier.

Chapter 5

The Guns Come to Toul

General John J. Pershing had been particularly anxious to create a distinctive American Army, but prior to the improvement in Allied fortunes in the summer of 1918 this had not been possible. In the preceding year Petain and Pershing had planned to transfer control of the line north of Toul to American control, but the serious situation created by the German advance in April and May had precluded this. Finally, on July 24th, Pershing was able to issue a formal order creating the American First Army, to take effect on August 10. This was done by the expansion of I Corps, which would have four American Divisions with two in reserve. I Corps was to be placed beside III Corps to form an American Army, and it was planned to transfer command from the French to the Americans on August 10. Headquarters of the new army were initially at La Ferté-sous-Jouarre but were transferred to Neufchateau upon its creation.[1] The British reluctantly agreed to the transfer of American Divisions that had been under the command of Marshal Haig to fill out the First Army that was to be under Pershing's command.[2]

August 12th.

In a deserted room on the top floor of an old stone barracks, I sit on a long bench studying French. For a table I have laid a board across an old rifle rack. With a great effort I keep my mind concentrated on the French book. It is very warm. Perspiration flows freely. The zooming flies play in the sunshine which streams through the high open window. They buzz about my head and crawl distractingly across the book page. Outside a great confusion of sound adds to my studently discomfort.

Dozens of trucks are roaring through the cantonment gates and ranging themselves in close packed rows about the parade ground. Men call to each other above the uproar. A motorcycle, pounding out its staccato note, races across the open space and disappears out of the gate. Overhead, eight aeroplanes are adding their music to the gasoline symphony in the yard.

47

Finally, the French book loses out. I go to the window and try to see what it is all about. Never before has my study hour been so greatly disturbed. What does all this racket mean?

The trees hide most of the parade ground, but I can see that these are French motor lorries. Very dirty and dusty they are, and several have broken down. They evidently have come a long distance. From the window I cannot see what is in them, and I am very curious. I can hear more of them coming up the road. Where have they come from? What does it mean? It is almost supper time, so I submit to my curiosity and run downstairs.

Begrimed Frenchmen are everywhere. Each machine as it comes into line seems to shake off five or six grease and dust men. Every third truck carries a wagon. No— what is it? There are wagon wheels sure enough, but all else is hidden under a tarpaulin painted in green and black yellow splotches.

Suddenly I see—I recognize the contour of the hidden object and a projecting muzzle—the famous 75's, dozens of them, and here in Toul while the great battle of the Somme and the Oise is at its height. It can mean only one thing, and I begin to search for other signs. Yes, the 1st and 2nd U.S. are on this front; reports have them "resting"; they came a long way to rest.

Then the 89th is here, and the 82nd, and the 5th is not far away. Moreover, there are other U.S. divisions on the front. Added to these a division of Algerians and a division of French and we have quite a little army. An army of easily 200,000 men to hold a quiet front, strange strategy. I look at my map. Where are we? Are these troops here just to rest up? It is far from here to the scene of the big battle. And what about these rumors I have heard? Big guns at Nancy. Sixteen inch guns at Pont-a-Mousson. Oh! La, la! There is going to be something doing in Alsace Lorraine soon.*

Meanwhile the Boche is getting his "Nase voll"** on the Somme and the Vestle, and rushing up every man available. Watch what happens when this U.S. First Army strikes?

— — — — — — — — — **M E T Z ?** — — — — — — — — —

August 15th

It is a lazy life we lead here. The American members of the P.T.B. were withdrawn from the Pexonne front on the second of August and came by truck to Toul, where the headquarters of the Radio Section is now located. On the way we stopped for lunch at Luneville, a pretty little town with a most interesting old cathedral. In a field not far from the road as we entered the town there was a peculiar little hut with a sort of kite frame above it. This was a goniometer post or wireless direction finder used to locate enemy wireless stations.[3]

It is a part of our service and the two operators were old friends who greeted us heartily as we came in. They showed us how we revolved the frame over the hut and charted accurately the direction from which the wireless waves were coming. Any enemy wireless station is quickly located by tracing the direction through a series of these "goniometers" along the front. Then the artillery makes it hot for the enemy operators.

---

* Note: Note the date of this entry. It was just one month later, on September 12th, that the St. Mihiel Drive began.

** Note: Nase Voll = German for "Nose Full."

On arriving at Toul we were quartered in these old French Barracks just out of town. Here, many friends of the Transport and Langres signal school greeted us. The place is alive with troops, and every evening the road leading down the hill to town is crowded with men on leave. During the day most of the troops are kept under cover.

Yesterday after supper, Peterson and I wandered into town. We went down by way of the field to the station because we wanted to see if there was any more activity. On the edges of the field some Algerian artillerymen were encamped. They lay sprawled on the grass in the shade of stately oaks which also shelter a half dozen short muzzled howitzers, wicked looking monsters. They were like gigantic green and yellow frogs, seated on their haunches, gaping at the sky.

The railway yard was a busy place. On one side were dozens of freight cars from which U.S. troops were unloading all the paraphernalia of batteries of 75's. Hundreds of horses and mules stood beside the tracks. At the other side of the freight yard were groups of sailors—yes, sailors, red tassel caps and all, way over on the eastern frontier of France. There were six ten inch naval rifles all camouflaged with pictures of playful sharks painted on the barrels. The sailors were putting them on heavy steel wheeled trucks of special construction. These trucks were hooked to powerful motor-tractors, which were hauling them up the road to our parade ground where all the rest of the French artillery is.

If "Jerry" should get wise as to what is in this quadrangle, he will surely do his best to make things lively for us. He was over again last night and dropped a few torpe-does, but I have not heard where they hit. That makes the fourth night in succession that he has visited us, not to mention twice during the day time. So far most of his attention has been to the station and aviation field but two bombs hit in town and ripped the front off several houses, killing two people.

From the station, Peterson and I went to the Red Cross hut and bought chocolate and read papers and magazines for awhile. Next, we visited the café on the corner and sat down to a couple of glasses of beer. Feeling greatly refreshed we proceeded down "main street" to the parked square just outside the ancient walled part of Toul. The picturesque stone towered gate and drawbridge were before us and we had to show our passes to an M.P. as we went through.

"Must be out of town by nine-thirty," the sentry warned.

The narrow cobbled streets were crowded with uniformed men. Most of the shops were still open but some merchants were bringing out the heavy board shutters and putting them over the windows.

There was a commotion in a doorway; a scolding woman's voice, which ended in a squeal. The door flew open and a buddy stumbled out and bumped right into us. He was a little the worse for wear but in the best of humor.

"The little blank—blank kicked me out," he grinned. "Pas de soldat ce soir, Hubby coming." He looked at the door regretfully. "Didn't kick me out last night. Come! Have a drink on me."

We entered the "American Bar" on the corner. Here was life indeed. White marble tables all crowded with men. Waiters could not keep up with the demand, but every-one was happy. The perspiring bartenders worked valiantly to keep from being mobbed and the red-faced waiters rushed among the tables with balanced trays while hands pulled at them from all sides. "Tout'suite." "Tout'suite." "Viens tout'suite." "Trois biere." "Oui!"

"Never get waited on here," commented our newfound friend looking at the crowded bar; "no place to sit down anyway. Let's go! Better place down the street. I'll show you the town."

He burst out the front door and stopped short. The unlighted street was very dark after the brightness of the Inn. He was mumbling something about "get by—it's a cinch." Out loud he said, "Come on, I'll show you fellows a real place."

At the next corner he turned to the left into the side street. It was not twenty feet wide, cobbled, inky dark and deserted. With slight misgivings we followed in the wake of our guide, who never stopped talking.

"T'aint very far—just a couple of blocks; lucky you fellows ran into me; I'm in the S. O. S.; been stationed here for two months and I know all the M.P.'s in Toul. When we get there, you all lay back till I call."

This was the oldest part of town. The houses leaned crazily over the two foot sidewalk and the cobbles sloped down to a single gutter in the middle of the street. We turned another corner and faintly the sound of laughter could be heard, with the tinkle of a piano.

"Stay right here," whispered our guide, "I'll be back in a minute."

Almost immediately he was back with an M.P., whom he introduced formally, after asking our names.

"It's all right," assured the M.P. "I'm around the corner—see? But remember—get out by nine thirty."

"Sure. Certainly," we agreed.

Our guide pounded on the door three times. An elderly Frenchman with walrus mustache and shiny bald head opened the door.

"Ah! Bien venu, bien venu Monsieur Martin!" He beamed in recognition.

"Yea! It's me, Papa," said our guide, "and I brought a couple of buddies along. Get us three beer, will ya? I been promising these fellows a drink all evening."

The door had closed. A hazy light streamed into the stuffy hall through the opening to the café where some twenty Frenchmen and some seven or eight Americans sat on benches about long heavy tables. Perhaps half a dozen girls were present, most of them serving drinks.

As we entered, a poilu with a violin climbed on a bench beside the piano and began to play and sing in a heavy alcoholic voice a plaintive French song which seemed to amuse his comrades

Papa, Keeper of the Café
Drawn from memory by father

immensely. It ended in deep mock pathos with the man acting the part of a rejected lover suicide amid much applause.

There were cries for the "Madelon" until the accompanist at the piano struck up that roaring tune and the violinist began to sing the first verse. The entire assemblage came in strong on the chorus. At each verse they became more enthusiastic until the leader was standing on the table, extending his arms like a traffic cop and the rest of us got up and waved our glasses to the stirring theme.

"La Madelon," I am told, has already reached the States and become the rage. I heard it first in Pexonne way back in May. The French of our service used to sing it to the accompaniment of Steinmeyer's guitar.

When the song was over, everybody ordered more drinks. Time passed very rapidly so that when presently I looked at my watch it was nine forty-five.

"Come on, we got to beat it, fellows," I urged, "or the M.P.'s won't let us by."

"Yea! We got to go," agreed Martin, "don't let the M.P.'s worry you, hick. Come on, I ain't scared of the M.P.'s; got to get back to quarters. That's all."

We were at the entrance trying to accustom our eyes to the darkness when the sirens began to shriek. What an unearthly noise they made. The wail of damned souls —the howl of all the devils in hell—there is no suitable simile.

"Shut that door," yelled the M.P. "and get the hell out of here as fast as you can."

"All right, Sid, old boy, we ain't lingering," said Martin, and just then he tripped over a cobble and sprawled in the gutter. What he said then is not printable. We picked him up between us and started down the street double time. At every corner the sirens roared in our ears.

As we approached the gate Martin collected himself, straightened up and walked to the M.P.

"My two buddies here got tied up with me. Don't see 'em, will ya?" He pointed at the sky as several searchlights focused on one spot.

"Off the street. Down in that cellar everybody!" ordered the M.P., paying no heed to Martin. He pushed us down the steps.

"Them sirens mean clear the streets," he explained.

We found ourselves in a low vaulted basement somewhat like a tunnel. Here were people, soldiers and civilians, a number of children and a woman with a baby which cried plaintively. An elderly hawk-faced Frenchman with a flickering candle on a bottle came down the stone stairs which led from the house above. He was followed by a bright-eyed boy of fifteen in a flapping night shirt, with an accordion under his arm. The kid danced across the dirt floor, a sort of highland fling, night shirt for kilt, the squeaking accordion drowning out the baby.

Outside the sirens had stopped and the humming motors faded. There were several heavy explosions, and then quiet. Presently the M.P. opened the door.

"All over," he said. "Get to your quarters as quick as you can."

We were walking rapidly up the hill to the barracks when a voice hailed us:

"OH! BUDDY! HEY THERE! WAIT a MINUTE—Don't make—me—run. WAIT!—I'm going—can't—lose me."

We turned to see a man come hurrying up the hill. He labored heavily and was much out of breath, appearing to stagger a little as he came toward us out of the gloom. Another drunk, we thought.

"You—fellows—going—up?" he asked, catching his breath and looking oddly past us.

He was a little man, not more than five feet, but stockily built, bandy legged and heavy in the shoulders. He did not wait for our answer; seemed to be talking to himself.

"The First's up there. I'll find the bastards. Hi, hi, hi, ha, ha!—Gad! I want to see Twister, the blank, blank, he'll think he sees a ghost."

"Gonna be a row," he confided, "Hell of a row—he, he, ha! Benny's coming! OH TWIST! G—— D—— him—thinks I'm out—no hospital kin hold Benny when that gang's going in—he, he, he! Damn it! How far is it! Just gotta find the First before this show starts."

He turned to us and began to plead wildly: "Don't ya understand?—first battalion—machine gun company—got bumped—Belleau Wood—hi, hi, hi, ho, ho, ho! WOW!—we give 'em hell—until—BLOWIE!!!" He stopped with a crazy joyful little chuckle, wiped his cap off his head and came close.

"Feel my head," he said, like a mischievous kid letting us into his secret, "easy now, don't tickle my brain."

My God! My hand drew back. Half the man's skull was missing. There was an irregular opening in the side as big as an orange. You could feel the edges of the bone and then the scalp drawn over the saucer-like depression.

"Hi, hi, hi, he! Hard head, ain't it?—woke up in the hospital four weeks ago—jumped it when I heard of this shindig. T'aint no hospital kin hold Benny wid that gang going in. They'll go to Berlin or Hell sure this time—come on, let's go!"

As the man carefully put his cap on again, he began to curse and blaspheme as only a regular knows how.

"Jesus Christ! Some blank, blank Boche is gonna pay for this blank, blank headache, or my name ain't Benjamin."

We were walking toward the barracks by this time and he never ceased talking.

"Bit light headed, but I'm au'right. Captain Blake'll let me stay if Twist says I'm O.K. Gad, I hope he ain't out—and Warts—that's my sidekick—son uv a blank, ain't no better man in the army—if they got him—!

His teeth gritted wickedly and suddenly he noticed that we had turned in at the gate.

"Hey! Where we going?" he asked, stopping short.

"Better stay over night with us," we urged. "It's getting late, Benny. Get a good breakfast in the morning and start out. Plenty of time to find your outfit. This show won't be on for another week."

"Sorry! Can't do it—got to be moving." He stopped as though listening. "Here comes a truck going my way—so long!"

He was gone. We heard him hail the truck driver as he had hailed us. I cannot get him out of my head; keep wondering what became of him. Will he find "Twister" and his gang, get bumped off happily in this show, or live miserably to peace?

Chapter 6

U.S. First Army Listening Station "Renard"

As every former serviceman knows, there are always those in the enlisted ranks who have some ideas about the big picture. On occasion these ideas turn out to be correct. However, in my father's case, he had information that was unavailable to the average doughboy. Also, by its very nature, the organization to which he was assigned gave its members a much greater degree of independence than would otherwise have been the case. As tension built, and rear areas became crowded in preparation for the coming Allied advance, it was necessary for him to rise to the additional responsibility which resulted from promotion.

At this point in the war, aviation activity and in particular balloon busting, had become very prevalent. Balloons were widely used by both sides in World War I to observe enemy troop movements and could be used to direct artillery fire. There was great motivation for enemy airmen to shoot them down, which was dangerous work indeed. Observation balloons were well protected by machine gun emplacements, and the explosion of suddenly burning hydrogen would buffet an attacker's aircraft and possibly suck it into the flames. The greatest American balloon buster was a German-American named Frank Luke who was killed by German infantry on the ground after having downed three balloons near the Meuse on September 29th and landing his Spad in spite of his wounds. I would speculate that the German pilot who downed three balloons in one morning, as described by my father, was either Oberleutnant Heinrich Gonterman, who was credited with twenty-one balloons during the war, or Oberleutnant Fritz von Roth, who downed eleven. The Pfaltz D III was the preferred airplane of German balloon busters because it could be dived harder and faster than the Albatross. This was probably the small German plane my father saw.[1]

August 2Ⅰth.

Back on the line again. I am writing this by the light of a candle fifteen feet underground. I have just relieved Weber at the apparatus. Here I sit at the old job of listening. Ohh! I'm sleepy. Weber woke me up. Went outside to stretch. A beautiful night, but a bit chilly, held a clear cold moon in a cloudless sky. To the north there were signal lights, four green stars following each other diagonally upward; southwest there were rockets and flares, and further off the rumble of cannon. Somewhere up in the blue, a flock of bombing planes returned from a night raid.

My Ingersol says that it is 2 A.M. This is the "Renard," U.S. First Army listening station. I'm in charge of post. It's a good position, all underground and camouflaged, in the middle of a daisy field, just opposite Flirey, on the St. Mihiel salient.

We get much enemy T.P.S. We made out five different stations today. They call every hour.

Our shift came up yesterday from rest quarters at Domèvre. We will be three days on post and will be relieved tomorrow. As yet I do not know the sector very well,

The author wrote on this photograph: "St. Mihiel Front. Listening Post 'Renaux' August 1918."

This photo is uncaptioned, but it probably is also of the "Renaux" because the building does not fit his description of the "Chasseur" and there is a steel tower, probably for the support of antennae, on the roof. These individuals cannot be identified.

although I had a good look around this morning. It is rolling, open country with here and there a patch of woods. I followed our wires along the Flirey road to where the overhead lines come down to cleats in the side trenches. A little further on they are hooked to a heavy insulated cable which runs through a culvert and is buried in the bottom of the trench. I hope to trace that cable to its end; I feel I ought to know where it is grounded. These cables won't be broken as easily as the old French loops were.

This photo was probably taken at the "Renaux" even though it is labeled "Pexonne P.T.B." It is on the same page of the photo album as the other photos, and the building does not fit the "Chasseur" description. It is likely that these are members of the Pexonne P.T.B., but photographed at the "Renaux." These men were all removed from the "Chasseur" at the same time. There are six men. Remember that Grubel was gone and the author was the photographer because he is not in the picture.

We miss the French cooking. There are only three of us, Weber, Morach, and myself. Morach does his best with corn-willie, canned beef and potatoes, but the meals have lost their charm. Mess kits have replaced china plates, and vin rouge bottles are gone but not forgotten.

This front is quiet enough. Since we have been here there has been very little shelling but the show in the air is on a grander scale. This afternoon four Allied planes were vertically overhead very high up, so high that they were mere specks against the clear blue background. Our attention was drawn to them by a popping noise in the sky. When we looked up we saw white streaks like slate pencil lines on a blue slate, and then the four dots glinted in the sun as they turned tails up.

"There they are," pointed Weber, "four coming straight down in a hurry. Something's after them for sure—Boche tracer bullets out of an empty sky—wait a minute, here they come, see 'em, pin points—1, 2, 3, 4, 5, getting bigger every second, must have been clean out of sight."

Five German fighting planes seemed to spring out of a clear sky, spitting dainty white threads, like spiders trying to entangle flies. They did not follow the Allied planes far down, but presently wheeled, took "V" formation, and started back toward their own lines. They were not taking chances with our antiaircraft guns. As soon as they turned, the guns let loose, but they were still very high and the batteries had no chance at all.

August 25th.

It is evening and I am sitting on a bench before our rest quarters in Domèvre.[2] The last rays of the setting sun shimmer against the aluminum painted observation balloon which hangs like a majestic sentinel, one thousand feet up just back of the town.

This little village is very old indeed. There is a great stone well in the center of a small square shaded by hoary oak trees. That well must date back through the ages, for the flagstones about it are worn concave by many feet and the heavy stones of the coping have great grooves in them from ages of dragging up the bucket ropes. Some of these rope grooves are over a foot deep.

At sundown the village swineherd comes down the street driving some thirty pigs and a few goats. The wrinkled and bent old peasant woman carries a long staff in one hand and a little curved horn in the other. Every hundred yards she blows the horn and the villagers open their doors to receive the returning livestock. The animals seem to know their homes for seldom are they goaded; two or three enter each doorway and run through the front hall to their quarters.

There is a new man among us by the name of Rosen. He is in the house now, talking as usual. A dapper little New Yorker, who says he landed in France ten days ago and made a quick trip to the front. He tells everyone he arrived last week, much as to say, "now let the war start." He was a professional dancing instructor in New York, and that perhaps describes the man better than anything else. Good humor and brass nerve are his salient qualities. He gets away with more devilment and special privileges than any other man in the outfit. He had hardly arrived in this metropolis before he located Lulu. Lulu Paolette Witte, known as Lulu of Domèvre, now takes most of Rosen's spare time. Whether she is teaching him French or he is giving her dancing lessons, we have not been able to discover.

The other day Rosen and I were out for a walk. At Manorville we entered a little French store. There was one small window, so dirty, and so filled up with onions and carrots and other wares that very little light penetrated. Also, the sun was setting and American doughboys were swarming into the place eager to spend. So eager that presently the stock of walnuts, grapes, raisins, figs and chocolate is "fini" and the boys are raising pandemonium, pricing every article in the store while the poor old French woman becomes more and more excited in fear that her stock will be pilfered. With the declining light, she lights a candle and places it on a box in the middle of the counter. Dozens of hands hold out articles from all sides and the boys yell, "How much? Combien?" until the poor woman tears her hair.

Rosen takes up a crook handled walking stick and thrusts it across the counter. "How much for the hockey stick?" he cries above the din.

Somebody throws an onion across the room and hits a fellow at the end of the counter. He howls for revenge and picks up the first item that comes to hand, a five cent baby doll, and lets it fly back.

With that the proprietress goes wild. She shrieks and jabbers and shoves at the laughing mob, "Saligauds! Allez! Tous Allez!"

"The hockey stick," persists Rosen, hedging over near the candle, "yea! All right! But gimmie the hockey stick first."

He holds the crooked end under the woman's nose and she storms at him, thinking he is doing it just to torment her. All of a sudden he sneezes violently and out goes the candle. We rush for the door as a near riot breaks out in the dark store.

As we walk out of town Rosen struts gayly with his stick for which doubtless our Uncle Samuel will pay. The woman will put in a claim big enough to double her stock.

August 30th. Domèvre.

For several days we have taken our meals at a little French eating house on the main road. It is a one story stone hut with rough beams for ceiling under a thatch roof. A portly French lady serves us, aided by her red-faced daughter. The shriveled up little husband lurks timidly in the background, puffing a long drooping pipe.

This evening supper was about over but we were still seated at the tables when the most violent and nerve shattering explosion I have ever experienced shook the universe. Dirt rained from the ceiling and one of the log rafters slipped from its moorings.

For a moment consternation held us rigid. I saw the little Frenchman turn as white as ash; open mouthed and wide eyed he clutched at his pipe. The next instant he upset his chair as he dove for the door jabbering inarticulate patois.

"Air Bombs" we thought as we rushed out; but the sky was empty. Not until we walked around the house and looked westward toward the setting sun, did we see anything unusual.

A half mile away there was the most peculiar atmospheric phenomenon. Dense clouds of dust and smoke billowed upward, and a little above them a great brown tinted vortex ring like a doughnut several hundred feet in diameter whirled skyward.

As we watched there was a second devastating detonation. Even at that distance the concussion was terrific.

"Ammunition dump," remarked a captain of artillery quietly. "They've been after it for two days. Knew they'd get it sooner or later."

And now I remembered the peculiar shell fire the Boche had been sending over. A single high angle gun fired every three minutes in an odd diagonal direction across the line, and never seemed to be shooting at anything.

Every night for a week the roads have been packed with ammunition trains, hauling up these shells, tons and tons of them, costing thousands and thousands of dollars.

But it is a mere incident. Preparations for the drive will be speeded now that it is evident that the enemy is getting wise.

August 31st.

And now old gusty September will be with us again, September and the Boche still in France. We will have to do some tall traveling to be in Hoboken by Christmas.

I went raving the other day; sat for an hour behind the big stone crucifix in the French cemetery and unburdened my heart to the dead. I found them to be most sympathetic listeners. The peace and presence of the place stayed with me the rest of the day. I seemed to make friends with them. We held a long consultation solving weighty problems, and always came to the same conclusion, that I am an ass and should be a buck private in the rear rank:

"Quelle Guerre!
Quelle Stupidité!"*

September 3rd, Domèvre.

Balloon raids were the order of the day. Three of ours were shot down. The last one was our sentinel.

We were in quarters after dinner when an aerial barrage opened up outside. We ran out. A very small German plane was tearing down straight as an arrow for the doomed balloon. Shells burst all around him but he never swerved. The balloon sank as the cable was reeled in to the pennant (about five hundred feet). The observers

---

* Note: (In longhand by Author) Quoting the French on the Pexonne front: "What a war! What Stupidity!"

tumbled out and sailed down under white silk umbrellas. Machine guns blazed away; they gave that Boche a regular shower of lead, but he paid no attention at all. He zoomed not twenty-five feet over the bag and then turned in a steep bank and roared over the balloon again as though to make sure of his game. A curl of black smoke rose and the bag began to sag.

At that very moment six Spads dropped like meteors from the clouds. At the same time three or four other planes arrived. The air was suddenly swarming with airplanes all mixed in a general confusion. The whole affair lasted less than a minute. The Boche ducked and twisted through the new arrivals. A big observation plane, that had no business there at all, tipped over on one wing and slid down through space.

I had run up the road for a better view. An American colonel in intense excitement was pounding the road with a heavy stick and cursing under his breath. He raised binoculars to follow the German who was down low streaking it for home with the Spads in pursuit. Presently he lowered his glasses.

"Well I'll be damned!" he exclaimed. "Three balloons in one morning and not a thing to show for it."

Believe me that Boche had the "guts." I don't know whether the other balloons were his work or not, but I shouldn't wonder.

There is a scarcity of potatoes to take on post with us. Last night Rosen went "pomme de terring."

"You expect me to eat out of cans all of the time." He was quarreling with the sergeant. "I'll turn into a tin can soon. I'm going to get me some potatoes. Weber, will you come along? Have you got a couple of sacks, Sarge?"

"Wait a minute, Rosen," said the sergeant. "Where are you getting these potatoes? You steal them from the French and you'll get yourself shot full of holes to say nothing about put in the brig. I'm not letting you go—see?—So don't come back to me for sympathy."

"Who said anything about stealing potatoes?" returned Rosen. "I want a burlap bag to clean my shoes on. Come on, Weber, let's go for a walk."

A few minutes later we heard them rummaging about among a lot of rubbish in the back yard and exchanging wisecracks on the high cost of living, rag men, and hoping the Frenchman didn't have a dog.

It was a mean drizzly night, dark enough for such a prank but not very pleasant for wallowing around in a potato patch. We waited their return with interest and wagered upon success or failure.

An hour later we heard a song of triumph as our two foragers came up the road. Stumbling into the light, a sorry sight they were. Soaking wet and mud-smeared from head to heel, a bundle of onions hanging from one shoulder and carrots from the other. On their backs were sacks of potatoes.

"What's the idea of turning your coats inside out?" I asked as they dropped their burdens. "God, what a mess!"

"Disguise, camouflage," they explained. "And we'll have clean coats outside tomorrow so they can't spot us. Boy! Now we'll eat."

September 5th, night on post, Renard.

The Boche made things lively around here today. They blew up a battery ammunition dump near our post and the place burned late into the night. One man was killed and six were wounded. Shells fell all around the dugout in the afternoon but mostly they were shelling the road which runs up toward Flirey two hundred feet to the right. Our overhead wires were broken all to pieces. We will have a nice job in the morning.

The whistle of the "H. E.'s" just gave us time to duck. I picked up three shell fragments on the steps. At sundown they were coming over every two minutes. One had hit just before a platoon of men appeared at the end of the road going up. Morach and I called a warning to them. How bewildered they were! They had never been to the front before and didn't know what to do. They didn't know whether to believe us or not and thought that maybe we were kidding them. Then the sergeant started to go on, but the high pitched whine of the next shell settled the argument. We ducked. When we came up there wasn't a soul in sight. Presently a head was raised cautiously here and there. Then several started back the road on the run. Others got behind trees. We laughed ourselves sick. If we had not stopped them, they would have been right in the spot where the H. E. burst. The idea got their goats. They came into our dugout and went ahead through the trench.

After dark and all night long there is a roar in the back areas like the traffic of a great city. During the day the roads are empty. At night they are crowded with ammunition and supply trains, artillery moving into close up camouflaged positions, men and wagons, and trucks, trucks, trucks. Miles of trucks end on end, without lights. No wonder the noise is awful tonight. I wonder if the Germans can hear it.

There is a change in the enemy organization; that is certain. Until recently our instruments have received many enemy calls and line tests; in fact we have been able to distinguish nine different stations and report the calls. Since we came on duty this time we have heard only two stations and these were very distant. Tonight I know that the wires are broken but yesterday they were not. Is the Boche moving out of the advance areas and covering the movement with artillery activity?

September 6th.

Got word this morning that I am a Sergeant. This cheered me up considerably and I have been right on the job all day.

Weber and I set out early to repair the lines. They were smashed badly along the road and we had a long job fixing them. The road is a bad place for wires because it is always being shelled. We talked it over when we returned to the Renard at noon, and I went out alone after dinner to look over the ground to the left with the idea of stringing a new lead.

I cut across the field to the west and struck the narrow gauge track where it runs through a cut and followed the rails forward. There were several branch lines running into patches of woods where new battery emplacements were being prepared. I went in and spoke to the men of a group of 155's. They arrived on the front only yesterday and have kept under cover continually. Coming out only at night, they are preparing strong positions and comfortable dugouts.

A little further up the track I came to a fill on which the track crossed a little valley. Here I stopped to watch an air fight between three German and several Allied planes. One Boche dropped very low with a "Spad" on his tail, machine gun spitting. I thought he was gone, but he straightened out with a roar over my head and the last I saw of the plane he was fifty feet up sailing over no-man's land, wobbling badly but managing to keep his balance. The man was either hit or badly scared.

Two French officers came toward me over the fill. They were earnestly discussing something, looking at dugouts, hunting billets for battery personnel, probably. They passed me and took a side path into the woods. I went across the fill and came to a city of dugouts in a cut. Each "abri" had a paper tacked on the entrance stating for what outfit it was reserved and how many men it would hold. Just beyond the dugouts, the tracks were smashed all to pieces and the way blocked by a wire entanglement.

I entered the trenches which zigzag forward along the edge of the woods. Judging by the number of shell holes, this would not be a good route for our wires.

In the new method of warfare, very few men are kept in the trenches. I came upon a working party digging new positions but saw no troops. The trench led along the Beaumont-Flirey road which had been blocked to traffic for several years, and then forward across grassy land all cut up by small gas shell craters.

Now, the idea came to me to follow our cable forward, so I retraced my steps a little distance and turned east in the lee of a rise in the ground. I went down toward the big Flirey railway bridge. This bridge was a beautiful structure of very artistic and graceful design. One end was knocked from its abutment and a few shells had gone through the iron work; otherwise it was little damaged. Under the bridge an infantry company was quartered in strong dugouts.

I went on down towards Flirey. This ground was more familiar to me. Presently I located our cable where it comes out of the culvert and was buried in the ground. Picking up a trench shovel, the kind the doughboys carry in their packs and leave lying around when they go out of line, I proceeded up the trench until I came to a fork. Here I dug in the bottom of the trench against the wall nearest the enemy. Nine inches down I struck the cable. Good; I pushed the dirt back, stamped on it, and went forward. Seeing not a soul, I followed the trenches with the cable lead in this way a good thousand feet before I came to the outpost.

In a deep cross trench were two squads with a sergeant in charge. I spoke to them quite a while and asked them if this was the last post, or whether they had sentries still further forward. They said that this was the last occupied trench and that the communicating trench led into No-man's land and was blocked by wire just a little way up.

The first wire was not much of a barrier, just a few rough frames with barbed wire wrapped crisscross on them. I climbed the side of the trench and took a peep forward. It was flat country with a slight rise toward the enemy. A strip of entanglement led to right and left from where I was. The ground was covered with stubble and badly cut up. A hundred yards or more toward the enemy I could make out another line of wire, and in the distance near the top of the rise, another belt. Several communication trenches could be seen in sharp outline zigzagging forward through this barrier and on over the hill. I had seen enough to know about how far I could go before I took a chance of running into the German front line.

After digging again to make sure the cable was still with me, I climbed over the barrier. Shovel in one hand, grenade with cap removed in the other, I now advanced cautiously, peeping around corners, looking down all the side trenches. I had gone for perhaps two hundred yards when I came to a regular labyrinth of ditches and burrows and tunnels; the old front line works, now completely deserted but still in good condition. A big *minenwerfer* shell or "flying pig" had landed full in the trench before one dugout and there was still evidence of gas in the deeper positions.

I spent some time exploring the place. The dead silence and the mysterious uncertainty kept my nerves at a high tension.

Finally, I returned to the communication crossing where I had entered. Again I dug up my cable and proceeded to follow it forward as before. There was another cross trench and then the second barrier, just as I expected. This entanglement was very much stronger. Great tangled masses of barbed wire filled the ditch, and wooden frames strung crisscross had been thrown on top.

Here I hesitated a long time, caution and curiosity struggling for mastery. I kept telling myself I was a damn fool for coming out there, and that, if I had any sense, I'd beat it back in a hurry immediately; and then—I take a peep over the parapet. I am now near the top of the rise; a broad strip of entanglement runs to left and right. Just ahead a board is stuck in the ground, painted half white and half red, the diagonal being the color line.

Curiosity finally got the better of the argument; besides, I had come out there with the object of locating the grounds to that line and I would be beaten if I turned back now. I pushed my shovel through the entanglement and worked my way over to the lowest point. I did it as quickly as I could. It did not take more than thirty seconds at the most, but thirty seconds is a long time, and my one thought when I landed on the other side was: "Has anybody seen me?"

If they had, if some watchful Boche at an advance observation post had happened to be looking that way at the moment I crossed, I would probably be S.O.L.—and reported missing in the morning.

With no time to waste, I felt that I needed to get out of there as quickly as possible. I hurried on, putting speed before caution. Fifty yards ahead was a cross trench, and again I had to dig. Digging fast, I missed the cable at the first attempt. It turned down the cross trench. Up the trench, around two corners, and there was the cable lead running down a timbered shaft. Twenty feet down there was water. I could see where the grounds were fixed in the mud on the side near the bottom.

Enough, I had seen what I wanted, and there was no reason to stay longer and had a feeling that the climate in the neighborhood was not conducive to long life.

I made the return trip rather hurriedly, as though someone were after me. It's funny how a man's morale will break down after his mission is accomplished and he is beating his way back.*

September 9th. Domèvre.

I had a wild ride back from the lines last night. This "show" is coming off soon now. Things are developing in a hurry. Our relief arrived at the Renard in a signal corps Ford truck, and the driver said he would take us right back.

---

* Note: (Typed on manuscript by Author)
I have noticed the same thing time and time again, with troops going forward and coming back through shell fire. Going up they walk steadily, pay little attention to the whining of shells even when they land close by, and take their chances with shrapnel, with little show of nervousness. Coming back they drop into ditches when shells come near, they walk hurriedly, they jump nervously at each explosion, and they go around dangerous places, or wait in some shelter until the bombardment stops. On the way back they are almost out of it and do not want to get "bumped off" at the last moment; they have nothing to think of but their own safety.
(Added later in longhand by author and still later crossed out)
I make no excuse for this expedition. It happened exactly as told. It was unnecessary and asinine. I submit it not as hero stuff but as a study in war psychology. It may well be omitted without loss.

Night was falling as we climbed aboard and I think that driver had a date. He certainly made a speedster out of that bus, and we three bounced around in the back like dice in a cup. We butted our heads and nearly bit our tongues off when we tried to talk.

Soon we were on the main road where the night traffic was all against us but the fool chauffeur never even slowed up. You couldn't see a thing; no lights at all and clouds of dust churned up by hundreds of wagons and guns and ammunition trucks. I just propped my feet across the back, held on to a post and prayed when I could keep my chin from bumping my knees.

Suddenly—"CRUM–M–MP." There was a crash of splintered wood; something hit me in the back and threw me head first against the opposite wall. For a moment I was dazed. There was a trampling of hooves and a neighing and squealing of horses. The Ford had stopped very abruptly, being impaled upon the shaft of a two horse French wagon. The pole had hit a board at my back and driven through.

Did those Frenchmen cuss? What they said I cannot repeat, but it was very expressive. They were just getting hands and arms to talking, when the tied up traffic became impatient. Dozens of hands lifted the Ford and untangled the horses. We climbed back in and were off again in no longer than it takes to tell.

That driver was not cured; the date must have been very urgent. We had gone less than half a mile and were speeding up a smooth straight road, our side clear but the up track on the left jammed. Presently—Bumpedy! bumpedy! bump! bump! bump!—I thought I would turn inside out. The driver had mistaken a narrow gauge railroad for a nice highway and we were taking the ties.

All out while he maneuvered back on the road. Now I was keeping my fingers crossed in anticipation of the third mishap. It came soon enough and was no worse than a roll down an little embankment into a field. This our chauffeur said he did on purpose in order to avoid hitting a truck. We put our shoulders to her and pushed Lizzie back on the road. She was steaming badly by this time and getting balky. In the outskirts of Domèvre she stopped dead and refused even another gasp.

"Out of gas," said the driver, and claimed the tank had sprung a leak. I was perfectly satisfied to take to man's most ancient mode of locomotion.

A long column of infantry was standing quietly at rest in the dark street of Domèvre. As we approached, commands were repeated down the line and the column got under way. They were turning up our road getting the old thrill out of the trap, trap, trap of many hobnailed shoes beating the road in unison. At our quarters we stopped and watched the column go by. Three or four companies had passed by when they halted again as long columns will.

"What division?" I asked the nearest private.

"Second, got a cigarette?" he returned with the usual request, licking his lips in anticipation. "Can't smoke now, want it when we get in. Thanks. Yea! Fighting Second —just up from Tigny but it ain't the same bunch. They ran us back long enough to refit and fill in with about 25% replacements and shipped us up here."

"Pipe down there, Al!" This came from the squad corporal who had seen the sergeant approaching.

"Expect half of us to get bumped here," continued Al, obeying the corporal to the extent of lowering his voice a little. "The rest they'll use up at Verdun."

"Shut up will you!" This time the corporal emphasized the words by poking Al in the seat with his gun.

I think Al was talking for the benefit of the new recruits. He was acting smart and incidentally letting out information to a stranger.

Presently they were ordered to attention and moved on.

We were turning in for the night. I was sitting on my bunk taking off my shoes. Outside, the division was still going by. Rosen had the floor as usual. He was demonstrating, with Shuster as victim, how he got his first army haircut and nearly lost an ear.

"He got me by the nose like this," he said, catching Shuster's proboscis in his left hand. "But he could get a better grip on me. Then he started his electric lawn mower through the middle of my hay field cutting a furrow to my neck—Z—Z—Zip!"

Just as he was demonstrating this stroke on Shuster's cranium there was a violent explosion, so violent the whole house shook and a window cracked.

Shuster jumped up like he was shot. Flinging Rosen ten feet from him to the floor, he yelled, "Put out the light!—Bombs! Put out the light!" Shuster was nervous and I don't blame him.

"Get under the bed! Get under the bed!" This sage advice in a high pitched voice came from Rosen who had already followed it. I am uncertain whether he meant it or was mocking Shuster.

Air bombs on a little village are no joke. In a big place you have some chance, they cannot hit everywhere; but in Domèvre, they could mess up the whole place with a few bombs.

Lights were out and we had crawled to bed. Outside, the marching column was still going by—trap, trap! trap, trap! trap, trap!—like a machine, soulless and inanimate.

My bunk was under the window. I had forgotten the cracked pane and was dozing off, when I felt a concussion and instinctively jumped to a sitting position. The action was so quick that when the glass fragments of the window fell, they landed on my empty bunk. I don't understand it exactly, I certainly jumped before there was any sound. Is it possible that the concussion arrived ahead of the sound? It is said, there are only two kind of men at the front, "the quick and the dead." Well I am quick, but I hope I am not getting jumpy.

This morning everything is peaceful again. The roads are as empty as ever. The troops are all hidden away in the woods. We took a walk around the countryside and visited our new balloon. The cable is attached to a reel on a truck with five machine guns set up in a three hundred foot pentagon around it. We kidded the gunners over the loss of the old balloon.

In the distance we saw Frenchmen working on a railroad track which led to four dead end sidings prepared long ago in the woods. The heavy railway guns will be brought up the evening before the drive.

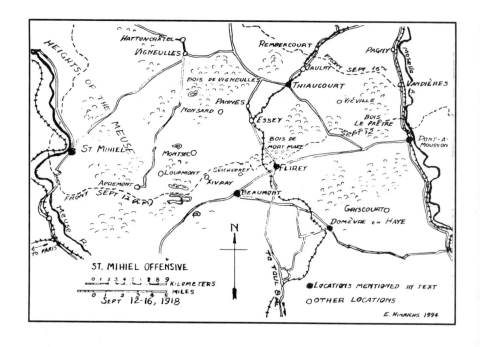

HEIGHTS OF THE MEUSE

HATTONCHÂTEL
VIGNEULLES
BOIS DE VIGNEULLES
PANNES
NONSARD O
ST. MIHIEL
MONTSEC O
O LOUPMONT
SEICHEPREY
XIVRAY
APREMONT
FRONT SEPT. 12 (A M)
MEUSE R.
TO PARIS

REMBERCOURT
JAULNY
FRONT SEPT. 16TH
THIAUCOURT
O VIÉVILLE
ESSEY
BOIS DE MORT MARE
FLIREY
BEAUMONT

PAGNY
VANDIÈRES
BOIS LE PRÊTRE
SEPT. 12
PONT-A-MOUSSON
GRISCOURT O
DOMÈVRE EN HAYE

N

ST. MIHIEL OFFENSIVE

0 1 2 3 4 5 6 7 8 9 KILOMETERS
0 1 2 3 4 5 MILES

SEPT 12-16, 1918

TO TOUL & R.R.

● LOCATIONS MENTIONED IN TEXT
O OTHER LOCATIONS

E. HINRICHS 1994

Chapter 7

"Tonight She Blows"

On August 12th (Chapter 5) when my father first observed the tremendous build-up of men and material in the ancient city of Toul, he had speculated that there was going to be a big "show" in Alsace Lorraine. While violent battles were raging in the north, a full month was needed before the logistics were considered sufficient by the Allied General staff to commence the St. Mihiel Drive. My father had predicted that the objective would be Metz and it is interesting to note that when General Pershing saw how successful the drive was, he was sorely tempted to go on and capture Metz. He did not yield to this temptation to continue the advance, since he felt that it would have diverted him from the ultimate objective.[1]

September 11th. Night on Post.

Tonight She Blows, A French lieutenant has his map spread out on the table beside me. His battery of 75's is lined up in a field outside. They arrived at sundown. You can hear the shells clank as they stack them alongside each gun. The lieutenant studies his map and I look over his shoulder. Ruled pencil lines spread fan shape from a central point and one line runs back through Beaumont.

"Pourquoi cette ligne?" I question in very poor French.

"L'observateur, il est a Beaumont," informs the lieutenant.

"Oh! Dans la tour de l'église, n'est ce pas?"

"Eh Oui!" agrees the Frenchman, smiling.

"A quelle heure commence le bombardment?"

"Une heure," he says in an offhand manner as he folds up his map, stuffs it into his pocket, and walks out.

I give my entire attention to the apparatus. The enemy is very quiet; he has undoubtedly withdrawn from forward positions, but our wires are entirely too active. Artillery lines are being tested, new Signal Corps stations are active and there is more telephone talk than there should be. Often there are several messages at once. I keep busy writing down everything that I can make out, especially the profanity.

65

We'll send it all to headquarters for the education and amusement of the intelligence staff.

Enemy listening stations can certainly hear enough tonight to take warning, if they have not already done so.

One telephone conversation I must give in full as I got it:

"Brrrr! Brrrr! Hello! Brighton!"

"Yea!"

"Jake! Message for Lieutenant Howard Watkins, Co. 'C', 106th Infantry."

"Yea!"

"It's a cable, special permit. Take it down."

"All right, let's have it."

"Eight pound boy arrived today. All well. Signed Bess."

September 14th. Toul.

The show is over and we are back at Toul. Time now to make a big entry.

At a little before 1 A.M. on September 12th, I left the apparatus and went outside. It was a very dark night; stars all hidden under heavy clouds; the front strangely, almost ominously, quiet. The 75's were ranged in a line across our field; gun crews lolling on the grass beside their guns. French wagons were still adding to the big piles of shells stacked by each gun.

An occasional flash followed by a heavy report back of the German lines was the only jarring note on a peaceful night. A few enemy long range guns were feeling out our back areas.

A group of officers at the end of the field were comparing watches; mine stood at 12'55, presently 12'57, then 12'58; most of the gunners still lolled on the grass, some apparently asleep.

Suddenly, there were several almost simultaneous brilliant flashes to the west which lit up half of the sky. Then as the heavy detonations reach us, two or three more flashes to the south. And now, within the space of a minute, the entire skyline was ablaze. Imagine a terrific thunderstorm in which the lightning flashes are continuous and in every quarter of the sky, and the thunder almost breaks your eardrums. The night flickered like a motion picture, and presently in this ghost light I saw that the road nearby was filled with men in marching column going into the front lines. Each figure a mechanical hunchback moving with the irregular jerky motion of the early films, shoulders bent forward to balance the pack. The artillery made such a deadening racket that the effect was that of silence. The senses were numbed to ordinary noises. The specters on the road seemed to move forward irresistibly in absolute stillness. They held my eyes fascinated, and for some reason the top of my head began to tingle. Hats off to the Doughboys! They are in the center of the ring; the rest of us are only seconds!

Now the French gunners begin to sit up and take notice. At the sound of a whistle they take their places. A few moments later there are five brilliant streaks of flame as the battery adds its burden to my already bursting eardrums.

For half an hour I sit on a boulder and watch the performance, nursing my ears now and then and becoming strangely more sleepy every minute. I'm in a daze, can't seem to control my thoughts, and keep yawning and staring at the black flickering sky, where dozens of shells like invisible express trains roar overhead at two thousand feet a second.

By two o'clock I am fed up. The bombardment is to continue until five. I tell Weber to call me if anything unusual happens and am glad to retire to our burrow where the racket is somewhat muffled. Strange as it may seem I fell asleep immediately, and slept soundly till dawn.

"Hey! Wake up! 5 A.M." Weber was shaking me. "They are going over. Nothing doing around here, Morach and I want to go up."

"Wait a minute," I say, sleepily, sitting up. The guns were still blazing away. "We are ordered not to leave post; may be recalled or something."

"Aw, we'll be back," urges Weber, grinning. "The wires are broken, see, and we are out fixing them."

We were outside by this time. Pale dawn was breaking in the east. Our battery still blazed away intermittently but the gun barrels were pointed at a higher angle. The road was jammed with traffic at a standstill.

Newly won ground has an irresistible attraction. The urge to go tugged at me. Here was an opportunity to visit another planet, so to say, and the only leash that held us was the chance of someone coming and finding the post deserted. With difficulty, I held the boys long enough to get breakfast: coffee, sardines, bread and jam. Weber promised positively to be back by noon, but I noticed that he stuffed a couple of pieces of bread in his pocket as he went off.

Now the French were hitching horses to the 75's. The war was walking itself away from me. By 7 A.M. I was alone. The temptation was too great. I also deserted post. I confess to it and hope to be forgiven.

On the road toward Flirey, I met the first prisoners; some fifty grey coated men in charge of two M.P.'s. A sorry looking lot they were, and I thought, "If this is all the material the Kaiser has left, the war is almost over." In Flirey another group was being lined up. These were certainly not first line troops, the poor quality of human material was too evident. Underfed, elderly, servile; surely a Reichswehr regiment sacrificed because they were useless.

I went on. Engineers already had repaired the road through the disputed area. Traffic was beginning to move again. All the paraphernalia of war was snaking slowly forward; field kitchens, supply wagons, engineer units, field wireless outfits, artillery and ammunition in endless array. Now and then a staff car, honking furiously, attempted to go by on the left of the line, but usually only jammed traffic.[2] In the old enemy front line several batteries of 75's were blazing away. I went on. The effect of the long bombardment was here very apparent. Huge shell holes on the road had been hastily filled in or the roadway had been deflected around them. A little further on a Red Cross dressing station had been set up, and several Germans were acting as stretcher bearers, stacking blankets and making themselves generally useful without any supervision that I could see.

Here I came upon the Lieutenant. He was sitting on a fallen tree whittling a stick between manicuring his nails. He had already discarded the pot helmet for the natty officers cap. Some five yards away on the grass lay a chubby faced kid in field grey, not over sixteen. The nearest American was over seventy-five feet away and paying no attention whatsoever.

The officer looked up as I approached. He was not a bad looking chap, of medium stature, bronzed, clean shaven, a type to be seen on any street in America.

"Guten Morgen," I said smiling amiably, "jetzt ist der Krieg für Sie vorüber, nicht wahr?"

He appeared not in the least surprised and smiled pleasantly as he returned my greeting and moved over on the log to make room for me to sit down.

"Max," he called to the kid who was his orderly. "Setz dich hierher. Das ist ja nett. Da können wir uns unterhalten. Ist viel zu sagen. Wo kommen Sie her?"

"Aus Baltimore," I said. "Und Sie?"

"Leutenant Thirlkel. Meine Familie ist in Frankfurt. Sie kennen Deutschland?"

"In neunzehn acht war ich da. Hab Verwandte in Frankfurt, Familie Fadé ist Ihnen vielleicht bekannt."

"Kenn ich nicht. Sind so viele, sind so viele."[3]

He was whittling away industriously now and seemed absorbed with his own thoughts.

Presently I asked, "Wissen sie wieviele Amerikaner schon in Frankreich sind?"

"Oh ja," he said without emotion. "Beinah' zwei Millionen."[4]

By this time one of the sentinels had seen us.

"Hey buddy! No talking with these fellows." Our conversation was interrupted just when it was getting interesting. I had to leave.

A quarter of a mile up the road a group of perhaps one hundred Boche had been herded into a ruined house and I took another chance. I greeted the nearest cheerfully in German. Hello! Here was a different spirit. Hostile, sulky, suspicious, they stared at me without answering. They had just come through a fight and probably had been roughly handled. Several were bandaged. They certainly were a contrast to the first lot I had seen. Even their uniforms were of better material. They appeared well fed, sturdy, spirited, and young. They began to crowd around me until I felt rather uncomfortable. I tried to overcome their hostility by being amiable and succeeded to some extent.

"The war is all over for you fellows," I said in German. "You ought to be happy. Soon it will be finished entirely. Do you know how many Americans are here now?"

"Over a million," the man I had addressed answered readily enough. "But that will make no difference."

He looked up at the advancing traffic on the road. "This will not end the war." He smiled scornfully. "Many times we have seen the same thing when we were going forward."

I noticed several of them whispering together and watching the guards who were at the corner of the house. One seemed to have something which he did not know what to do with. They came up to me and I heard one say:

"Gib' es ihm. Der ist gut."

They crowded around so the guard could not see and the man, a sergeant, pulled a piece of paper out of his pocket and placed it in my hand just as the guard ordered me away.

"Nehmen sie das—Souvenir," the German said. "Mir wird es doch weg- genommen."

I hastily stuffed the paper in my pocket and backed away. No one had seen the transfer.

It was now about eleven o'clock and I was getting worried about being away from post so long. Something seemed to be urging me back and I was burning with curiosity to take a look at that paper.

When out of sight around a bend in the road I took out the paper and spread it. Whew! Here was a find. It was a detailed military map of the salient, dated September tenth, less than two days off the press.

It extended back almost to Metz, and had peculiar little pennants all over it. I stuffed it into my pocket and hurried back to post double quick. The field was now deserted. I tumbled down the stairs to our burrow and with great relief found everything as I had left it.

Spreading the map out on the table I began to study it more carefully. It was the map of a special service, that was certain. What all the flags meant puzzled me.

I had been back less than five minutes and was reading the German inscriptions when there were voices outside and then footsteps on the stairs. Hurriedly I folded up the map, stuffed it in my pocket and took up the receivers, pretending that I had been on the job all morning.

In walked Lieutenant Thompson, beg pardon Captain Thompson, as I noticed. With him were a Colonel and a Major. All were in high good humor over the success of the drive, but I thanked my lucky stars they had found me on the job.

"Hello Sergeant! Where are the men?" asked Thompson immediately. "You are to dismantle station at once. A truck will be up for the apparatus by 2 P.M."

"The boys will be back," I assured him, "they went out a little while ago to make a repair." With that I pulled the map out of my pocket, hoping to divert his attention.

"Here is something that may interest you," I said casually, handing it to him and turning to write down a report which was coming over the newly established lines of communication:

"Our patrols continue to move forward rapidly meeting little resistance. The 1st Battalions reports advance lines in the vicinity of Pannes, all objectives having been taken" ———

The Colonel and the Major watched me write this down with great interest. I was going on when Captain Thompson interrupted.

"Say! This is interesting," he said, indicating the map, "where did you get this?"

"Off a prisoner," I said carelessly.

I could see he was curious, but he tactfully asked no more questions. He simply smiled and put the map in his pocket.

That Boche would have torn his hair had he known that his precious map would have been delivered to A. H. Q. G-2* before sunset. He could not possibly have picked a speedier channel.

"Have everything ready to put on the truck at 2 P.M.,"ordered Thompson a moment later looking steadily at me and smiling pleasantly. "You are all to report back to Toul tonight. Truck will take you right through!"

With that parting shot the three officers stumped out, leaving me not a little worried about those two sight-seeing boys of mine. Would they come back in time? I doubted it, and the prospect of having to dismantle station alone and lug everything out to the truck was not pleasant. It was nearly noon, so I prepared a little coffee and beans and went outside in the field to eat.

---

* Note: (Author's Handwriting) AHQG-2 = American Army Headquarters Intelligence.

Very peaceful it was here now. The midday sun shone warmly down between beautiful silvery cloud banks. The war had walked itself nearly ten miles away. Cannon still boomed in the distance and the road remained cluttered with traffic. Presently I began to laugh. This whole affair suddenly struck me as extremely funny. It was comic opera stuff. Two men go A.W.O.L. to the scene of battle; a prisoner delivers a secret map directly to Army Intelligence, and I sit lazily in a field eating beans and admiring the September cloud effects. "Quelle Guerre! Quelle Stupidité!"

The truck arrived late in the afternoon. I persuaded the driver to help me get the amplifiers and accumulators aboard together with our personal belongings, blankets, mess kits, tools, etc. Then I left a note on the table telling the boys to get back to Toul as quickly as possible.

* * * * * * * * * * * * * * * * * *

This morning at breakfast, in the barracks at Toul, I mentioned to my neighbor that Weber and Morach were still lost.

"Who is lost?" he laughed. "They're upstairs sound asleep. Couldn't wake 'em up."

I finished eating and hurried up to the bunk room. At the end of the hall two forms lay side by side in utter relaxation; dead to the world, mouths open, snoring peacefully. They had not even stopped to undress, had kicked off muddy shoes, removed jackets and thrown themselves down. Weber's big toes stuck from his worn socks. I gave them a healthy pinch. He mumbled reproach, rolled over on his side without opening his eyes and continued his even breathing until I shook him roughly.

"Hey, you!" I said sternly, "snap out of it, you're under arrest for desertion of post in the face of the enemy."

That worked like a charm. His eyes opened wide and he sat up. Then he saw me laughing at him and immediately slumped down again. But I had him awake now and did not intend to let him off.

"Say, what time did you get in?" I asked.

"About 12:30, Auh—Hi!" he yawned and began to stretch. "You certainly handed us a surprise at the Renard."

"What did you expect?" I asked. "Did you think I'd have your supper all prepared and waiting for you?"

"Well, we got in there about sundown," he grinned ruefully, "had been going steadily since daybreak. I thought we were due some eats and sleep. Hell of a shock to find everything cleaned out. You didn't even leave us a piece of bread or a blanket."

He acted as though this were a real grievance and began thoughtfully to examine the blisters on his feet.

"Serves you right," I said, "you're lucky if you don't get put on kitchen police for the rest of the war."

"We got a worse jolt when we found Domèvre quarters cleaned out too," he continued. "Then we did begin to get scared. Caught a truck, luckily, which brought us right through to Toul in record time. It was a long day and we hadn't been to bed the night before."

With that he yawned again and rolled over to go back to sleep.

"Yea, so it was a long day," I persisted. "What in hell were you doing all that time? Why didn't you come back as you said you would?"

He began to laugh and finally sat up and rubbed his eyes.

"It's a long story, Sarge," he said sleepily. "Hey, Morach, you bum! Wake up and help me out."

With that he tossed a shoe and hit Morach in the stomach.

"We didn't expect to go so far," Weber continued. "You see, we ran ourselves ragged trying to catch up with the infantry. Those fellows were moving, and they had two hours start on us."

"Boy, that's pretty country over there, neatest little towns and villages, not much busted up either back of the old front. We went miles, until we didn't know where we were. We could hear machine guns and rifle fire just ahead but never seemed to catch up to it. Horned in on a company mess for lunch and then took the road again. About two o'clock we were approaching a little village with a party of engineers when suddenly things began to get lively. Rat, tat, tat—zing—zing! The party scattered in a hurry and Morach and I edged along behind a stone wall to the front of the house. It was locked and barred. We went around back through a pig pen and got into a protected corner just as Fritz began to lay down a barrage on the road and town. When the bumblebees and hummingbirds begin to sing, Morach kicks in a cellar window and slips through!"

"Auh! I did not," interrupted Weber, half awake. "The window was already busted, I just knocked the frame out."

"Anyway," continued Weber, "it didn't take us long to drop in. Dark and cool it was after the bright sunshine."

"And the air smelled like sour wine," reflected Morach, "kind of stale, sour, sweet."

"Yea! And you," continued Weber, "start groping out instead of waiting to get used to the dark, then BING! I hear a blow and you let out a howl like you were shot."

"Well, damn it!" put in Morach, "I didn't see that pitch fork. Stepped on the prongs and the handle came up and hit me on the head. I thought I had been black jacked."

"Go on, tell the rest, soldier boy," urged Weber, "I'll check you. Did you pull your .45 and shoot the enemy?"

"I just fired one shot into the darkness," admitted Morach, mournfully rubbing his feet.

"Three or four, you mean," corrected Weber. "You were so scared you emptied your gun and busted about two dozen bottles and made the rats run for cover. About that time my eyes were getting used to the dark and I could see two barrels and stacks and stacks of empties but nary a full."

"Took me to spot 'em, didn't it?" said Morach, "way back in a corner under a bale of hay." His eyes were shining at the memory.

"Yea! And if the H.E. hadn't hit the roof, you'd have been there yet. Lord! You ought to have seen his face, Sarge! Eyes popped out of his head when the masonry began to fall, but he hung on to that bottle. The back wall crumpled down against our window and blotted out the light."

"Gawd! It was dark!" put in Morach. "If it hadn't been for sure fire—." He pulled out a little brass lighter and stroked it affectionately.

"It took a lot of coaxing and cussing but you finally did get it lit," acknowledged Weber, "and then we groped our way to the stairs and found the bolted door at the top. We had the door almost off the hinges when there was a lot of hollering and running and commotion outside and we didn't know whether it was the Boche or our men. Then a machine gun began to blaze away in the back yard and a couple more in the street.—Right there Morach decides that the cellar isn't such a bad place and we go back and open a couple more bottles—."

"The next time we come up, the door flies off its hinges at the first kick and somehow we are not scared of anything. The rear of the house is badly smashed and we crawl over the masonry out into the yard and stand blinking in the sunshine, Morach humming a little tune and clicking his empty automatic at the hill. Then a funny popping and singing noise starts and bits of stone begin to jump around us."— Here Weber paused as he caught sight of Morach doubled up with his head between his knees and shaking with silent laughter.

"What's the matter with you? Ain't I telling it right?" asked Weber. "What's so funny about it anyway?"

"Nothing at all," returned Morach, controlling himself, "you're doing fine. Don't let me stop you. I just couldn't help laughing. The machine gunner pokes his head up out of the pig pen and yells, 'Get down you damn fools! Down!' and you just stand and stare at him. If I hadn't pulled you off that stone pile—."

"You did not," interrupted Weber, "I beat you to the pig pen and you fell on top of me when you landed inside."

With that Morach doubled up again. "The gunners thought we were hit," he sobbed. "They rolled us over looking for wounds and then kicked us in the pants, and went back to their gun."

"A fine pair of hoboes you turned out to be," I said. "If you're telling the truth, it isn't your fault you got back safely. You owe that to the providential protection bestowed on all drunks. Today is Sunday. Better get up, come to church with me, and thank the Lord."

To my surprise they took me up. Eleven o'clock saw the three of us treading the flagstones of Toul's medieval cathedral. The church, though not especially large or ornate, was very old, possibly dating to the twelfth century. The marble flooring was worn deep by the feet of countless worshippers. A barefoot shaven monk was taking collection. He was aided by a big bellied man dressed like a medieval town mayor who tapped the marble flags before each pew with a tall steelshod, gilt-headed staff. Ahead of the monk walked a little girl dressed in white who carried a sort of cornucopia for the receipt of alms and a bouquet of lilies of the valley.

It was so warm when we came out of the church that we went down to a lonely spot on the Toul canal and stripped and plunged in. This greatly amused several girls promenading with escorts on the opposite shore. My wrist watch got a ducking.

September 15th.

Prisoners continued to come back. This afternoon about a thousand in one group were marched up the road toward the prison camp. The small guard of M.P.'s kept them going at a terrific pace and the Heinies were clearly all in. Many made desperate efforts not to fall behind.

Several times I called from the side of the road, "Wo kommt ihr her (Where did you come from)?" They did not even turn their heads but labored on, running, staggering, limping and sweating to close the least gap in their files.

Finally a tall, slim fellow, hatless and with his coat on his arm, came opposite me. He was in slightly better condition than his fellows and looked up at me with a wry smile when I spoke. "Thiacourt," he croaked in a barely audible voice, licking parched lips and wiping his face on his sleeve. No wonder they were all in. Thiacourt is over twenty miles away![5] If they had kept up that pace—.

The end of the column came opposite me. Here agony was written on many faces. The weaker men, through sheer physical exhaustion, had gradually fallen to the rear. Many were wounded. There were numerous bandaged heads, hands and arms. But they did not struggle. At the very end came three men in a group; a tragic sagging figure in the center held up by two comrades. His countenance a haggard grey green mask, the center man's feet moved like an automaton that needed rewinding. A few more jerks and they began to drag behind in the dust. His comrades bore him limp for five yards and then lowered him face down to the road, and, without once looking back, hurried forward to keep up with the column.

"I can't do it, it's murder," says the M.P. "We got orders to shoot stragglers, but, God, I didn't think it would be like this. Can't do it, that's all."

A medical officer pushed through the crowd. He turned the man over and saw that he was more dead than alive.

"I'll take charge of this man," he said. "Get back to the column, M.P. I'll be responsible."

The relief on the M.P.'s face was comical to see.

Part III

Preface to Part III

This final section of my father's account of his experiences in World War I is not as detailed or as well organized as the earlier ones. As with the earlier sections, only minor corrections in grammar and syntax have been made to the original manuscript. With the destruction of the St. Mihiel salient, there was a resting period for the U.S. First Army. As preparations were made for the final drive into Germany, more and more deception was used by the Allies. The General staff did not want Ludendorff to feel free to remove his forces from the area south of Verdun and to apply more German pressure in the violent battles in the north. The ruse was even carried so far as to dupe American Major General Omar Bundy into believing that he was preparing an attack on a thirty mile front with a paperwork VI Corps to force a passage through the Belfort Gap.[1]

Chapter 8

Souilly, U.S. First Army Headquarters and Old Friends

Every serviceman knows that the military life is one of the "luck of the draw." I think that this became evident to my father when he encountered wounded from his old regiment which had been in violent fighting in the area of Malancourt. It is of interest to note that the company commander of his old outfit, Company D of the 313th Infantry Regiment of the 79th Division, was an individual named Von Kennen who had been a private in his squad while training at Camp Meade before the Army classification system sent him to Camp Vaile because of his knowledge of German.

September 22nd, Souilly, U.S. First Army H. Q.

I am writing this in a cozy little barrack standing by itself at the edge of an orchard on the side of a hill. From our front door we have a beautiful view across verdant rolling country. Two American railroads run up the valley, and in the distance are the large canvas hangars of a very busy aviation camp. At all hours of the day the air is full of aeroplanes. They chase each other around like gnats in the sunshine.

Yesterday, we came by truck from Toul over the newly liberated highway along the west bank of the Meuse past St. Mihiel. The control of this road and the Toul-Verdun railway was the chief objective of the St. Mihiel Drive. We could see the trenches running along the hills down toward the town and there was much wreckage along the way.

How long we will be here I don't know. The U.S. First Army is taking over the Verdun area from the French. For the present we are in charge of Adjutant Godart of the French P. T. B. in the Verdun area. He won't bother himself much about us. This is the life; a sector pass and nothing to do.

We are eighteen of us in here and mighty crowded. Last night, most of the boys slept on the floor. I was spreading my blankets when Rosen came in with two collapsible canvas cots. He'd been on an expedition down the valley and commandeered one for himself and one for me. A handy man to have around is Rosen. When we had settled ourselves and things had quieted down a bit after the light was out, he reached over and handed me a doughnut and a bunch of grapes.

"Where'd you get the cots?" I asked.

"There's a big hospital a half mile down the valley," he explained and added quickly, "they were not occupied, they've got 'em stacked up by the hundred."

Today Rosen has stuck to me. He is in my squad now and is the hardest man to say "no" to that I ever saw. This morning we went down the valley and he knew all the girls in the Red Cross hut by name. They put us to work rearranging and putting up more tables in anticipation of a big rush in a few days.

The hospital is a great, rambling, rough wood structure, still partly under construction; one of those mushroom war buildings which grow with each new emergency. It is almost empty now but the staff is making preparations for heavy business to come.

September 26th, Souilly.

Still bumming around and getting rather tired of it. The French say we can do nothing on an active front and are perfectly willing to sit still and wait. We, being somewhat newer at the game, are getting restless.

As I write, the big guns are booming again to the north. There has been a continual rumble all over that sector since about two o'clock this morning. We knew something was coming off and have been impatient at being held here so long. That may sound like Blaa, but the A.E.F. has not been in this thing long enough to get tired of it, and the American morale is at a higher pitch that it has ever been.

The news gets better and better. If this keeps up, the war will be over and we will not even have justified our existence. Golly, I am beginning to talk like a flag-waving recruiting sergeant: "Every one must do his bit." It is in the air and it is infectious. Something big is happening up north. History is in the making within sound of our ears, and we have to sit here and do nothing. Oh, well! I probably don't know when I am well off.

September 29th.

Wounded are coming back by the hundreds. We have been trying to make ourselves useful at the hospital, carrying stretchers, helping the Red Cross serve these poor devils cocoa and sandwiches. My God! Such sights! Here is where one sees the seamy side of the war. Many men of my old Division, the 79th, are coming in.[1] After dark, truck after truck arrived piled crisscross with wounded on stretchers, one row lengthwise on the bottom, another crosswise with ends on the body sides of the trucks. The drivers said that they had been forty-eight hours on the way in a drizzle.[2] The distance is not so great but the roads are jammed and often impassable and they had to go carefully over the rough spots for fear of shaking these human wrecks to pieces. Many of them, when lifted out, certainly looked more dead than alive. One man's face was covered with blood and his uniform stiff with clots. I thought he was dead, but it turned out to be blood that had dripped on him from the man above.

The receiving room of the hospital was soon full and they overflowed into the Red Cross and the Y. M. C. A. Minor wounds had to wait as the surgeons worked feverishly hour after hour trying to keep up with the incoming tide.[3] Mud-caked, rain-soaked and blood-stained men lay silently row on row, patiently waiting their turn.

Suddenly, a kid in the corner began to rave. He kicked and screamed and then cursed violently as he was given the needle.

Many of these were Marylanders and I looked for the buttons of the 313th. There were several of "A" Company and more of "B" and then I came across the most dejected kid I have ever seen. Pale as a ghost, smeared with grime, he sat against a wall and stared before himself as though in a trance; 313 "D" was on his collar button and he nursed a bandaged hand.

"What's the matter, buddy, downhearted?" I asked. "'D' is my old company. I was with them for two months at Camp Meade. How is everybody?"

He looked up a moment gloomily and then continued to stare at the wall. "They're all dead," he said listlessly, "gassed and shelled—nobody left."

"Aw, cheer up." I said, "probably not that bad. You'll find nine-tenths of them in hospital. Men don't die that easily."

He shook his head and looked as if he were about to burst into tears. He was the most forlorn kid imaginable and I patted him on the back and tried to comfort him.

"Where did you leave them?" I asked.

"Up near Malancourt,"[4] he said, frowning a little and looking at his injured hand as though to collect his thoughts. "Captain Reilly[5] had left us two hours before; gas got him with a lot of others."

"Reilly," I exclaimed, "he was 1st Lieutenant when I left Meade."

"Von Kennan had charge when I left 'em," he continued.

"Von Kennan!" I repeated. "He was a private in my squad at Meade."

"Well, he was top sergeant when we came over and in command when I left 'em. All the officers were out—nobody's left now—all dead!"

I could not shake him out of his dejection and so left him wrapped in gloom, convinced that all his comrades were no more and not comforted at all in that he had escaped with a minor hurt.

October 5th, Souilly.

Still waiting. Nobody seems to know anything. The adjutant says that he is await-ing orders. We've been here two weeks now. Nothing very interesting has happened. There have been two air raids on the aviation field and yesterday a German observa-tion plane flew over so high he might have escaped notice, but some keen-eyed observer spotted him and soon the sky was speckled with little black and white puffs of bursting shrapnel.

The usual redistribution of the month's pay has been in progress the last few days. The "bones" have been rolling merrily day and night, and as I write, a Black Jack game is in progress at the other end of the room. Sergeant "Scotty," the Belgian, raked in most of the francs in the crap game this afternoon, but I believe he is delivering his winnings over to Rosen tonight.

"Scotty, Sergeant Bergholts, was in Belgium at the time of the German occupa-tion. He claimed U.S. citizenship and got away with it, served with the British for a year, was gassed and laid up for several months, and then transferred to this service. Short and stocky but rather sickly looking, "Scotty" must be approaching forty. A trifle crude, somewhat foul mouthed, with a horse laugh at every dirty story, "Scotty" is losing philosophically.

The other two men in this game are Privates Schenck and Lens. They are new men. Schenck is in my group. I should judge him about twenty-six. He is good looking, dark complexioned and has a little black mustache. He thinks he is a devil with the women. A former New York newspaper man; he was probably a good reporter. Very free spoken, Schenck loves to tell of his experiences and, if half his stories are true, he has crammed a lot into a short life. In New York a wife and two year old wait for him, but that in no way cramps his style over here.

And Lens—"Pigeon Lens" of Youngstown, Ohio; a small town, a home product and an honest, open character. He is big and fat and weighs over two hundred. At times he is childishly confidential with mother written all over him. This is his first time away from Youngstown for any length of time, a girl is waiting for him at home. He owns a lot and there will be a marriage when he gets back. No women or wine for Lens, but strangely enough, Schenk and Lens are thick friends.

October 10th.

At last we are going out. Orders came in this morning. My group and Sergeant Holmes. Full field equipment. The men are packing kits now. There's no room for this notebook. I will leave it in the barrack bag with the rest of my surplus junk in charge of M. S. E. Johnson in the French store house here. There will probably be no time to write anyway. Don't know what's ahead nor how long until next entry. From all accounts it will be lively enough. Here are our orders. I'll copy them. They may be interesting someday.

Robert Loghry
Major, Sig. Cps.
Radio Officer
1st Army

Secret
Army Radio Station
Memorandum #8

Am. Ex. Forces
H. Q. 1st. Army
October 10th, 1918

Detachment of listening station personnel,
Radio Section, S. C. #1, will leave here and proceed to the vicinity of Nantillois and Cuisy for the purpose of locating listening stations.
The duties of these detachments will embrace the following:

(a) To endeavor in every way possible, to intercept enemy telephonic or T.P.S. messages, by cutting in on lines running into enemy territory. This is to be done by bunching trunks leading to the enemy lines through your amplifier to ground; connecting your amplifier in series with lines from enemy territory; and cutting into pipelines; railroads and especially narrow gauge railroads as these frequently pass near Artillery P. C. S. from which point there is generally much T. P. S. and telephonic communications. If conditions will permit, to run out grounds leading to enemy territory similar to the usual practice with listening stations. You will use your own initiative in devising other means of obtaining information.

(b) In addition to intercepting enemy conversation you will take whatever steps are possible to police our own lines. Your equipment for this purpose is limited, due to lack of transportation, but should be sufficient to secure results.

(c) You will inform all men of your detachment to keep a lookout for cable leads run in rivers by the enemy for the purpose of intercepting our communications.

(d) The information which you obtain in this manner will be recorded on listening station blank forms. Matters requiring immediate attention to be brought to the attention of the nearest commander at once.

(e) You should bring to the attention of those concerned the importance of lines running to enemy territory being cut ahead of our lines. Otherwise, the enemy could intercept through induction or direct conversation within our own lines.

(f) An Army telephone central is located at Montfaucon and is connected directly to Army Headquarters.

Robert Loghry
Major, Signal Corps
Radio Officer
1st. Army

Chapter 9

Active Front, Cuisy, Nantillois, Cunel

While the orders of the First Army Radio Officer in his October 10 order were perfectly understandable and justified, their practicality under combat conditions turned out to be an entirely different matter. In his entry of September 26, Sergeant Hinrichs had commented that the French, in their experience, had said that nothing could be done on an active front. In the fortnight covered by this chapter, attempts were made to set up a listening post, but it turned out to be totally impractical under combat conditions. Since my father had left his notebook in his barracks bag at Souilly, his account of his experiences on this active front are probably less complete than some of the other sections of this book. (See author's note, page 84.)

October 24th, Souilly.

Two weeks! God! I've lived a lifetime. Am I glad to get back to this book! Weeks crammed full of experiences that stand out in memory with razor edge sharpness. I have learned the meaning of Verdun mud, flooded shell holes, stinking woods, streams of wounded under shell fire, villages cluttered with dead, attacks and counterattacks, barrages, and machine guns and snipers. For ten days I gambled with death, morning, noon and night. Again and again, by slim margins and odd tricks of chance, death passed me by. I have had enough of tempting fate and am well satisfied to sit tight right here in Souilly, heroics be damned, until the end of this dirty business.

Those orders! What a joke they seem now! Some job to put up to a group of irresponsible youngsters on one of the most active points in the line at the very moment when Pershing's First Army is delivering blow after blow and the Germans are counterattacking desperately to prevent the closing of the pincers in the direction of Sedan.

A wild goose chase we were on at best, with the odds all against us. The French Adjutant, speaking from past experience, had told us that we would be able to do nothing. Our officers doubted and determined to try.

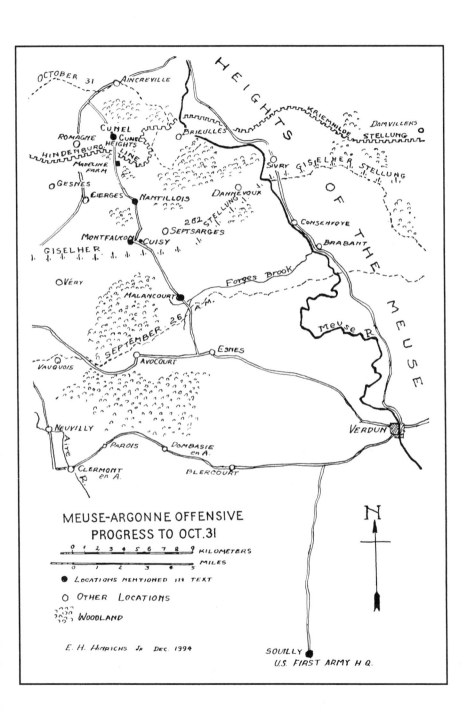

MEUSE-ARGONNE OFFENSIVE
PROGRESS TO OCT. 31

0 1 2 3 4 5 6 7 8 9 KILOMETERS

0 1 2 3 4 5 MILES

● LOCATIONS MENTIONED IN TEXT

O OTHER LOCATIONS

WOODLAND

E. H. HINRICHS JR DEC. 1994

SOUILLY
U.S. FIRST ARMY H.Q.

N

On October 11,[1] we set out in a truck for Cuisy, a little battered town east of Montfaucon. The Meuse Argonne drive had paused for a few days to allow the heavies to catch up and to permit a reorganization of the newly won ground. Mud! I thought I knew something about mud. Verdun mud makes you think you had enlisted in the Navy.

We picked out a little half buried shack about three miles from the lines and had hardly unlimbered our packs before—"Whiz Bang!" It sounded as though I could have reached up and caught it; she ploughed up the dirt on the hill opposite and made steaks out of four horses.

Small matter, our "heavies" all around us were singing a consoling tune. One baby in particular roared up and across that valley. She fired every five minutes and every time you'd think the boat was torpedoed or the sleeper wrecked.

None of us slept much that night. Water dripped and oozed into our shelters, the floor was hard and it was cold. Schenk, one of the new men, admitted later that he hadn't closed his eyes. He said that he never suspected that gun shocks could be strong enough to shake him in his blankets so that he had to hold on to keep from rolling off the earth. There were shell holes all around our quarters in the morning and some were certainly beauties. We heard afterward that our shelter had been occupied by an artillery P. C. but the Boche had made the place unhealthy.

In the morning we packed all our junk into the French cart and set out toward the line.*

     * * * * * * * * * * * * * * * * * *

After two days of dodging shell fire and lying in shell holes waiting for barrages to lift, we gave up the attempt to set up a real listening post. The amplifiers, batteries and spools of wire could not be transported and set up in a different place every day with shells falling like rain.

The third day Private Willman developed mustard gas burns. Private Herring who got the same gassing followed him to the hospital a little later. Then Corporal Keller of the original Pexonne P. T. B. got worse. He had been feeling badly for some time as a result of the gassing, but he thought he would work it off. Now he developed a temperature and was itchy. He went to the infirmary in the evening.

On October 15, I decided to leave everything except a buzzer set in the hut at Cuisy and go up alone to Cunel. When I announced my intention, Rosen insisted upon going along. I had seen enough of him to know that he was game and that there was no saying "no" to him.

The sun had risen clear that morning and warmed us pleasantly as we skirted the slope of Mont Faucon where artillerymen were already digging out the big guns for another forward movement.

---

*   Note: (In longhand by Author and probably added later)
Unfortunately my notes written at the time here become very unsatisfactory. They are very meager where they should be most complete. I was back at Souilly only three days, hardly time to get "decootietized," rest up a bit, and write a few letters, before we went out again on another expedition which later absorbed all my interest.

     However, perhaps it is just as well. A detailed account of our activities during those two weeks would add nothing to what has been told before. There are plenty of wild accounts of fighting activity which far surpass any of our experiences. The doughboys did the fighting and I am content to let them have the glory.

An ammunition train of Nash Quads had finally gotten through a badly broken stretch of road in the valley and came rattling up behind us. We clambered into the leading truck and sat on the bouncing shells as the driver jockeyed our bucking mount, with the peculiar weaving motion of these vehicles, around enormous shell craters and through sucking quagmires of sticky mud. The quad steers and drives on all four wheels and takes on a crab-like gait, the rear end switching around sideways as though trying to overtake the front.

In good weather the enemy had a clear view of this ground and harassed all our operations in this area with a nasty flanking fire from the east bank of the Meuse, which remained in their hands. Shells spattered the fields continually and presently a direct hit on the road ahead tied up everything. I was not sorry to get off that drunken load of T.N.T. and proceed into Nantillois on foot.

There was not much left of the town. Only gaunt skeletons of houses and piles of masonry. We took our places in the H. Q. mess line which had formed in a sheltered spot and then sat down to eat on the edge of a heavy stone water trough which had been knocked from its mooring and lay somewhat up-ended at the side of a ditch.

A shell shrieked by to the right and exploded a hundred yards off amid an avalanche of masonry. Several more shells fell and the streets were now deserted but three fellows were eating breakfast in the ruins of a house less that a hundred feet from us in the direction of the explosions.

One man, clearly visible through the doorway, was stretched out in the lee of the battered chimney. He figured that place just as safe as any other and did not intend to have his meal disturbed.

I had no sooner heard the screech of the next shell before I had vaulted the horse trough. I landed in the ditch as the shell exploded. The concussion was terrific and flying fragments whirred overhead. When I looked up, the house down the street was like the crater of a volcano. The shell had landed square in the center of it. Masonry had flown in all directions and a dense cloud of dust and smoke filled the interior. Terror-stricken men were running from the scene paying no attention to the groans that came from within the building.

I credit Rosen with grasping the situation and acting immediately. He had dropped into the empty trough behind which I lay. Now he jumped up and shouted: "There's a man in that building! Get that man; don't leave him there!"

With that we were running toward the house. The front wall had crumpled down in the doorway. So Rosen jumped through the nearest window opening, hesitated for a second and disappeared. I reached the ledge as he jumped in. Blinding dust and smoke filled the interior and there were peculiar crackling flames over the floor. No wonder the man hesitated. In the corner to my right were several cases of small arms ammunition knocked topsy-turvy by the explosion and right at my feet the ground was strewn with rifle shells. In that fraction of a second I saw little tongues of flame leaping among the splintered boxes and heard the crackling of the burning fragments. Then, I jumped down and trampled everything underfoot.

The groans came from a pile of bricks against the far wall. Rosen was already uncovering the man's head and presently we had him clear of masonry. He was badly cut up—head, face, shoulder, hand—but the worst injury came to light when we uncovered his legs; one knee joint was completely ripped off. I ran to the street calling for a stretcher. Just as a fellow came running up with one, an ambulance raced up the road. We tried to stop it, but it would have run us down and gone on, had it not been for a fallen wire which came into the driver's face. He put on the brakes swearing at the wire and us.

Nantillois

When my father was under combat conditions he did not have his camera, and he didn't have time to buy postcards. I have made this illustration based on the information in the text.

Ernest H. Hinrichs, Jr.

"Can't stop; got a man in here," he snapped, pushing the wire over the roof of the car.

"Don't give a damn. We got another! Just a second."

We had that man on the stretcher and in that ambulance before the next shell whined. They were dropping them one every forty seconds or a minute. It went high, two hundred feet or more from the road.

Now the ammunition began to go off wholesale. Rosen and I shook hands. We both felt very happy. It was the first time I had forgotten myself completely. The truth is, after I trampled out the burning ammunition, I forgot all about it. I didn't think about it again until we were running up the road and the next shell whistled.

We did not stop to finish breakfast, just packed up our kits and beat it up the road toward Cunel. The embankment to the right was lined with French and American guns. They had been put in position during the night. The contrast between the French and American digging operations was so marked that I asked the Americans why they didn't dig in.

"Oh! What's the use?" the man I spoke to said. "We won't stay here long, and if the Boche start shelling, we'll get under the guns. That trench and these holes are just for inspection."

The Americans had the most dangerous position near the top of the hill where the Boche shelled constantly.

I saw them every day for a week, but the last time I passed they were still sleeping (most of them) under shelters half rigged over cubby holes, dug into the bank. Meanwhile the French had gone down into the earth in several places ten to fifteen feet; all had roomy dugouts with benches and tables. Even so they were not satisfied and the dirt was still flying. Those men had learned from experience, they were taking no chances.

At the top of the hill the road forked to the right toward the Ferm de Madeleine and Cunel. An ammunition truck was standing at the fork and four men were unloading cases of 75's and stacking them by the road. The men were fuming and cursing and grumbling, but sticking to their job.

"What's the matter?" we asked.

"Matter!" snapped back one of them. "Orders, G—— D—— 'em! Ain't this the hell of a place to put this stuff? Some damn fool at headquarters looks at a map and picks this as a convenient spot for ammunition."

There were no trees or houses or cover of any kind on the hill; open country stretched away to the east where in the distance enemy observation balloons could be clearly seen.

"This is our second load. Got two more to come," puffed a sweating red faced fellow as he dropped a box containing a dozen shells off the back of the truck. "We'll bring 'em up all right, but they won't stay here long."

Two shells had whizzed by and hit within one hundred yards of the road as he was talking. Now the bombardment doubled up and things began to get most unpleasant. The last case was pulled hurriedly off and the driver clashed his gears and stepped on the gas as the men climbed on the back. The next instant Rosen and I dropped flat on our faces. The higher the pitch the nearer the mark. It is said that the one that hits you is not heard at all. This one was a few feet too high, it struck fifty feet beyond the road.

We ran the other way and then I spotted a hole somebody had been kind enough to dig. It wasn't much of a hole, two feet wide by four feet long by two feet deep. My diving experience came in handy.[2] I was on my face in the bottom when the next one hit. The hummingbirds this time sounded more like a swarm of bumblebees. The swarm had hardly passed before Rosen landed on top of me. We wriggled around until I got my face out of the mud and we could sit up and look at each other.

Another shell dropped near the crossroads and there stood "Buddy" number three at the edge of my hole pleading for room. He dropped in on top of us as the next shell whistled. She hit with a tremendous crash. Our bathtub rocked but the sides could not cave in; we were wedged too tight. Several cubic yards of earth flew overhead. I shall never forget Rosen's face within three inches of mine, eyes like saucers and the oddest little grin.

I: "That damn thing hit close."

Rosen: "Just twenty feet short."

I: "God bless the fellow who dug this hole."

Rosen: "Damn good hole, Hinrichs, but not a health resort."

I: "Let's get out of here."

Rosen: "O.K. by me."

Two more shells whizzed by and then we took our heels up the road. It is a queer sensation to have a shell come five miles and drop that close, making a hole ten feet across, but it is surprising how little it worried us. We ran up the road several hundred yards until out of the bombarded zone.

Now the nature of things changed. Here the road was empty except for scattered parties of men on foot. This ground was all newly won. Streams of wounded and prisoners were coming out and the dead were unburied. The further we went the more dead there were. A half dozen tanks had been disabled as they rushed a patch of woods at the end of a field. A nauseating odor assailed us. The thicket was full of German dead, machine gunners who had dug their own graves. But they were recent; the stench came from decomposing horses just off the road.

My father probably drew this picture of "Stinking Woods" from memory while working on the manuscript for this book in the early 1930's.

There had been a counterattack, for back of the woods we came upon several filled shell holes with American helmets hanging on crosses of splinters. On one splinter I read this pencil scrawl:

"Hier liegen acht Amerikanische Krieger."*

Beyond the stinking woods the road went straight forward across open country for several hundred yards. Here a line of American wounded on stretchers carried by young Germans were coming out. As we approached, the foremost pair set down their burden and the other stretcher bearers followed suit. Then, they pulled thick slices of white bread from their pockets and began biting into them like starving men. The first aid station just ahead had given them the bread and they were stopping to eat on this exposed stretch of road.

"Hey! Buddy!" the American on the first stretcher called to me weakly. "Let's move —!"

"Get you bad?" I asked, coming close.

"Side," he said quietly but in evident distress, "bad enough, but two back there got to get to hospital or they won't last."

Did I make those Germans jump? Wide eyed, they snapped to attention when I ripped into them with a line of German cuss words I didn't know I possessed. I have to laugh when I think of their scared faces with mouths choked with bread that they dared not chew. Probably they had been sworn at with more professional skill but never with more enthusiasm.

"First to the hospital," I ordered as they picked up their burdens, "then you can eat."

As they marched off without looking around, I wondered how far they would go before their hunger tempted them to another bite of bread. I had a feeling that they would stop again as soon as I was out of sight.

Just ahead was a thicket of trees and a rough timber barn, Ferm de Madeline.[3] Here a first aid station had been set up and the surgeons were doing a rushing business. Several hundred men were about the place. Field grey uniforms mixed indiscriminately with the olive drab. German stretcher bearers scoured the woods for wounded.

Two tall, lean fellows in dirty grey came toward us in the bend of the road. They carried between them a stripped sapling from which hung an improvised hammock holding a doughboy who looked more dead than alive. They had picked him from among the corpses on the road side.

As we reached the second bend, the road turned through the thicket and continued up; we noticed that we had the place pretty much to ourselves. Only one youngster was going our way.

"How far is it to the line?" I asked him as he joined us.

"How far?" he looked at us with an odd expression as though he doubted our sanity.

"Come on, you'll soon find out."

We rounded the bend and a beautiful little valley came into view with the road running straight across it. Wooded hills at the far end formed a background for what had been a picturesque little village. Now, a sinister spell held this valley in its grip.

---

* Note: (Typed by Author) "Here lie eight American Warriors."

The village appeared to be bubbling as in a cauldron. A cloud of dust and smoke hung over it. It was literally being beaten to pieces before our eyes. We had gone less than two hundred feet from the shelter of the woods when we began to feel very much alone. As far as I could see, we had the valley to ourselves, but a lot of devils with chattering teeth were mocking us from the cover of the hills.

Then suddenly the air became alive with singing hornets—zing—zing—zip.

"Scatter," said the doughboy, and he ran off the road to the left. Rosen turned to the right and I chased after him. He dropped into a large shell hole in the middle of the field about one hundred feet in front of a clump of bushes. As I came sliding with an avalanche of gravel down the side of the crater, Rosen sat sprawled out on the muddy bottom laughing at me.

He shook the mud off one hand and then off the other and carefully wiped them on the front of his jacket, all the time giggling like a school girl.

"Ha! Ha! How far? Did you say how far, Hinrichs?"

His laughter was contagious. We spent the next few minutes sitting opposite each other in that hole, wiping off mud and laughing at ourselves. Every now and then we would peep over the rim and try to decide who was shooting at what and whether that row at the village was a German or an Allied barrage. Suddenly a couple of one pounders (37 millimeter guns) began to pop out of the clump of bushes behind us. There was no smoke but we were able to spot them definitely by the sound. The wicked little shells went zimming over our heads and we puzzled our brains to decide what their target was.

For two hours we remained in that hole, watching the invisible giant, Mars, grind that beautiful little country town to pulp.[4] Those sturdy stone structures, centuries old, did not go to pieces easily. The needle pointed church steeple was hammered again and again but it clung miraculously to its foundations, battered and scarred and rent by great cracks.[5]

We got hungry. It was now 1 P.M. by my Ingersol and our breakfast in Nantillois had been interrupted. Rosen opened a tin of emergency rations and we dined on hardtack and water and discussed our next move.

Toward mid-afternoon the drum-fire on the village stopped abruptly. A number of men could be seen working forward along the edge of the thicket to our right and then more came into view near the edge of the village and in the ditch along the road. Things were much quieter now, so we left our shelter and went back to the road, keeping well separated and taking some shelter from the depression on the roadside and the row of tree trunks. A phone lead had been strung here and we considered the possibility of tapping but found the wires broken again and again.

We hurried on toward Cunel, drawing rifle shots from the woods whenever we stopped without cover. Nothing makes a man madder than the "Pop-Tsing" of a sniper's shot. You hear the bullet go by a few times and you boil over with rage against the man behind that gun. The "Pop" came from the woods three hundred yards away and we would be lucky to hit a man at one hundred feet with our Colts.

We entered the east end of the village and at first the dead appeared to be in sole possession. They were everywhere, mostly German but also a sprinkling of American. It was uncannily quiet in the place and as we went from house to house we felt decidedly lonesome. Presently we came across a single doughboy sitting, rifle in hand, crouched up under an arched cellar window. He stared at us sullenly as we passed. The second house behind him had a very strong cellar which remained in-

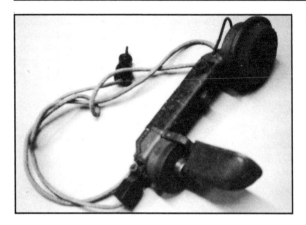

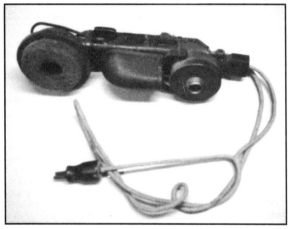

German Field Telephone the author picked up near Cunel. The small button on the handle had to be depressed to talk.

tact. Here were a dozen or more of our boys, keeping close under cover and waiting. It was at least comforting to know that the place was occupied by our men.

Near the center of the town we came upon the enemy headquarters. There were many wires which we traced to their ends. The telephones were ripped out and there was a sign on the door:

"Schreibezimmer der Kommandant."

Here was much confusion, smashed furniture, a litter of papers and some maps in a broken desk drawer. We pocketed these although they seemed of little value.

Out in the street again we followed some wires west. One entered a large stone pipe in which lay a dead German. I picked up a field telephone beside him.* At that moment there was a rat—tat—tat, tsing—tsing—tsing as machine guns began to sweep the street. Rosen and I beat it into the nearest house. We nearly fell over two dead Germans lying on stretchers, one with his stomach ripped open, the other with the top of his head gone. The four stretcher bearers, who had attempted this rescue, we found a few minutes later, crouched down under sheets of corrugated iron in the rear of the house. They had all been caught in the general destruction of the American barrage.

I did not like the sound of those bullets sweeping the street and the few live infantrymen in the place were lying too close under cover to be reassuring. At any moment the enemy might open up a counter barrage. We could not find one hundred feet of wire intact, but we did find a three bulb radio amplifier broken up in a ditch. Rosen picked it up and we began to work our way along the rear of the houses toward the hill. We came upon a mine-like doorway before a flight of stairs leading under

---

* Note: (In longhand by Author) I brought this telephone home and still have it. See photographs on this page.

ground. There was a strong dugout ten feet down. It looked dark, damp, cold, and empty.

"Looks good to me," said Rosen, throwing his bundle of maps and papers on the floor and reaching for a cigarette. He sat down on the old amplifier box, and began to examine the maps he had thrown on the floor. He exhaled a great cloud of smoke as he uncovered a map of Ypres and vicinity.

"Not much good now," I remarked, "except maybe it shows where these fellows came from."

"If we could set up our apparatus here we ought to get something," I mused, examining the place more carefully as my eyes got used to the gloom. There was a lot of refuse and old equipment around. "A strong dugout, close up, and in a key position, just what we want."

"How are we going to get the batteries and stuff up here?" Rosen asked suddenly. "Lucky if we get ourselves out."

"We might bring 'em up tonight," I suggested, "and run out our wires before morning."

"Oh yea!" he exclaimed, without looking up as he pulled a letter and a picture out of an envelope.

"Here's a letter from the Oberleutnant's lady friend. She sent her picture but I notice he didn't keep it. Not bad at that—. He studied the features closely and then pulled a photograph from his own pocket and then compared the two.

"Ground our wires over the hill," I continued thoughtfully. "Make an ideal post."

I stopped to listen and then ran up the steps to the entrance. Something was happening on the hill. A plane roared over not a thousand feet up. The stuttering machine gun and rifle fire doubled up in volume.

Rosen had come up beside me and we were standing uncertainly in the doorway.

"Not so good," he said, squinting at the plane, which wheeled over and went down out of sight behind the village. "Let's move,"he continued, "before something happens. I've done enough sight-seeing for one day."

Chapter 10

Camouflage Expedition to Verdun

As Allied pressure increased against the Germans in the north, the General Staff wanted to keep them guessing as much as possible about Allied capabilities in the area of the great fortress of Verdun, site of the tremendous battles of 1915 and 1916. The Germans had twelve divisions concentrated in this area and it was important to preclude their being moved to the north to reinforce their forces there. As part of the deception, personnel from the Radio Section were sent to the Verdun area to create fictitious radio activity. The idea was to delude German listening stations in the area as to Allied intentions.

October 30th, Souilly.

I got back last night from a most interesting three day excursion. We were all alive with "cooties" and had to go through the delousing plant this morning. If what they tell us is true, we earned our keep this time. At any rate we were in on a big game, how big, history will tell.

Last Saturday I was writing at the Evacuation Hospital, when Kaplan tapped me on the shoulder.

"Hinrichs, you're wanted up at the store room," he said, "Lieutenant Benjamin sent me down to get you. There's something doing; I believe we are going out again."

We hurried up the hill to quarters and almost bumped into the Lieutenant coming out of the doorway.

"Sergeant," he said, "get your things packed immediately. A light pack is all you'll need. I have given Scotty all the dope. Holmes has a map for you. As soon as you're ready, hurry over and get something to eat."

With that he started off down the path as though he had to catch a train. I ran into the barracks and nearly fell over Lens, who was busy rolling his pack on the floor just inside the door. Schenk was at work on a similar job just beyond him.

"Where are we going, fellows?" I asked.

"Don't know," grunted Lens, struggling with his pack straps. "Seems to be a hurry call."

"How many of us go? Where's Scotty?"

"Only seven, but all three sergeants. Don't know what's become of Scotty—hasn't made his pack yet."

Here Holmes came up and handed me my map. I began flinging questions at him, but it was no use. He just grinned. Said that he didn't know any more than I did.

I spread out my map. It was an intelligence map of large scale, almost two inches to the kilometer. I did not at first recognize any of the places shown. The opposing trench systems were represented in red and blue. The defenses of the enemy down to the minutest detail, every outpost, every trench, every battery position. Only the first line of our own was marked and the entanglements. Finally I spotted some familiar names and knew that I was looking at a map of the country east of the Verdun.

Then I made my pack, ran out to the mess hall, gulped my food down and hurried to the garage, only to meet Willman and Lens and to be told that the others had departed in the Ford touring car, leaving instructions for us to wait for the return of the car. Willman said they had taken no amplifiers, only two buzzers.[1] I got out my map again and we studied it. The Ford would hardly make the round trip in less than two hours and it was now after one o'clock. I went back to look up the Lieutenant and found him at mess with the Captain. I asked to be enlightened, but was simply told that Scotty had "all the dope." He added, however, "You will operate one end of the line and Holmes the other. I want something to come over that line tonight without fail, and the earlier the better." Then he smiled mysteriously and wouldn't say another word.

"Yes Sir," I said. I was "seeing in a glass darkly."

I went back to the garage and waited around an hour or so, talking to Willman. Finally the Lieutenant came along. Now he was in a more talkative mood. He was jubilant at the prospect of adventure, and had dropped all formality. He said our part was not the whole of the game, he was coming up with us to see the fun and was going to work a spark sending set. I asked whether it was an active front. He said he thought it would be lively enough, at any rate the Boche had "beaucoup" artillery and twelve divisions concentrated opposite in expectation of an Allied attack. Then he added enthusiastically:

"If they keep them there a few days longer, they will be out of luck—S. O. L. and it is up to us to keep them there."

I let out a long whistle, this was big game indeed, much bigger than I had expected. I was getting kind of worried over prospects of getting away with our hides. To be bumped off in the closing act of the war did not exactly appeal to me. I couldn't help thinking of where I would be that night. The Lieutenant said we were to wait for him at the radio station in the citadel of Verdun. Half an hour later the Ford returned and we were off.

We sped along the great Verdun boulevard, wide enough for four cars abreast and crowded with motor truck convoys, all going about thirty miles an hour. It was this road that had saved Verdun in 1916. We passed huge supply depots with their mountains of food and fodder covered with camouflaged tarpaulin. There were great stacks of ammunition and seemingly an inexhaustible supply of food for the ever active French 75's. There were several batteries of six-inch rifles on heavy rubber tired trucks drawn by two powerful gasoline tractors. All were camouflaged like Zebras in yellow and green and black. Overhead an "escadrille" of Spads roared by, flying low on the way home from the front.

Finally, we crossed the Meuse and approached the old walls of the fortified city of Verdun. In the arched gateway an M.P. tried to stop us because we had no pass. A little explanation and persuasion and he stood aside and told us the way to the citadel. We rolled through the tunnel and took the road up the hill to the right which led straight to the old fort. There was a deep dry moat in the sides of which were built underground quarters for thousands of troops. On the surface were many barracks of stone construction, badly smashed up but not completely destroyed as I had expected they would be after four years of bombardment.

We located the radio station. It was an army station operated by men of our section; I knew most of the fellows of the post. We immediately went upstairs and bummed some eats; it was four in the afternoon and we did not know whether we would get another chance. The cook handed out a delicious feed of cooked apples, fresh biscuits, and real butter. I had not tasted biscuits for months and, as the cook said to go to it, we stuffed. It was a good thing we did, for we ate but little the next forty-eight hours.

At about four-thirty the lieutenant arrived in his side car and ordered us to go ahead, but to have one man, who could operate a spark set, on the road to meet him where the Ford turned back. We went straight through the city of Verdun and up on the famous heights to the east. To my surprise the front was very quiet. Our artillery was almost silent and the roads were deserted.

It was evident that there were very few troops in the sector. This puzzled me. It was so entirely different from what I had expected. We had heard rumors of a big American drive to come east out of the Meuse to liberate the Briey coal fields and outflank Metz. Even the military experts in the papers had pointed out the possibilities of such a move. The unquenchable Rosen had had the plan of operation enthusiastically explained to him by a French major.

The road led almost due east for some six kilometers. As it approached the last ridge, we could look down over the country beyond; a flat open plain with small patches of woods. There were several villages visible in the foreground. Once they had been villages; now they could more correctly be called piles of brick.

There was dilapidated camouflaging along the road here and presently we came to two stakes driven in the way to block passage. A wagon trail ran down the hill to the right.

The driver said to Scotty: "Shall I go down? They came across with shrapnel last time but I'll drive the old Lizzy to Berlin if you say so."

"Sure, go ahead," returned Scotty. "We got packs and the place is over a kilometer away."

The Ford rattled over the loose stones down the grade. It had gone more than halfway and was already in the valley when Holmes appeared in the middle of the road with his hand outstretched as though to catch us. His face was wreathed in a wide grin.

"Whoha!" he said. "You fellows are looking for trouble. The town is absolutely deserted; you can't go on down. The whole valley is under direct observation. Get the Ford out of here."

"We got all this wire and stuff," argued Scotty. "Let's go down to the end of this stretch anyway. Looks all right to me."

The place certainly was peaceful enough, a regular sleepy hollow. Heavy brambles and bushes everywhere and the road was the merest trail.

The car began to move forward again as the driver released his brakes.

Suddenly there was a sharp report down the valley and at almost the same instant: "WHIZ—BANG!"

Right there that driver changed his mind. He made a world's record for an "about face" on a narrow road. Everybody tumbled out, bag and baggage, and then he put the old bus through a hill climbing test that would have decided any prospective purchaser. The sparks flew. She put her tail between her legs, made a noise like a scared mule, and raised the dust. It was comical; Jerry's observers must have rolled over with laughter.

When the Ford had gone, Holmes told us that they had reconnoitered the place thoroughly. There was no infantry in the neighborhood, the trenches and dugouts were all empty, the only defense being two machine gun posts, one on either side of the valley. That was not much comfort, for the valley was easily a half mile across, with a labyrinth of trenches, to say nothing of the ruins of the village to afford shelter to inquisitive patrols. Of course, the machine gun nests would have to be taken before any advance up the valley could be attempted on a big scale, but enterprising patrols could filter into the valley without meeting resistance. The place was spooky; it made you talk in whispers.

Holmes led the way into a trench which we followed for several hundred yards, finally coming to a big strong dugout in the hillside. Here we met Scotty, Pete and Schmidt. It was already getting dark, so we had no time to lose. Holmes went himself to help the lieutenant work the spark set.

There were bunks for eight men in the dugout, but they were full of old straw and very dirty. Pete had been busying himself with a little tin stove in an effort to make coffee, but the stove objected strenuously, and showed its resentment in the form of voluminous smoke which drove us out of the "abri."

When the "gas" cloud cleared, I got after Scotty and demanded the "dope." He read me his orders and several other papers of conversation. I could not get a copy of the orders but the conversations I kept and will bring home with me. We were to run out half a kilometer of wire, hook a buzzer and ground to each end and send fake messages to each other so as to make the enemy listening stations believe that there was an increase in activity. We knew, of course, from our own experiences how the American buzzer stations operated, how they made their line tests, and the kind of calls they used. For the night we would confine ourselves to test calls every two hours. The field service instrument is a buzzer and telephone combined.[2] In the morning we would get in a few telephone conversations. A glance at the map will show that Eix is on the main road to Etain and the railway runs out through the valley. The very fact of the absolute silence was what made the Germans suspicious. Troops could be rushed up from Verdun and beyond overnight; a heavy attack could be launched in the morning. The first evidence of such an impending drive would be signal corps activity throughout the region with an increase in wireless activity and code communication between Army, Division, and Brigade Headquarters. This part of the program was being covered by the stations at Verdun and the lieutenant's spark set. Then there would be a sudden increase in buzzer activity in the lines with possible telephone talk close up to the front. Such an increase in signal corps activity, in case a big attack were impending, might be detected several days before the time set for the zero hour if the enemy listening and intercept stations were on the job. We had every reason to believe that they were very much on the job in this region.*

It was almost dark when we began laying our wire. Pete and I held the spool on a stick between us and let the line unwind as we moved forward. Scotty and Lens were the other two members of the party. We followed the trench leading forward from the dugout for a very short distance and then came out on an old narrow gauge track running along the side of the hill. The rails had all been smashed to pieces long ago. We followed it forward in silence until we came to a belt of barbed wire. Here we set down our load and held a whispered consultation. It was quite dark by this time. The only sound was that of a distant bombardment to the north.

Finally, we left the rails and ran our wires down the hill along the entanglement. Scotty went ahead and explored the way. Pete and I with the spool followed and Lens brought up the rear. We stumbled over hidden bits of wire and threaded our way over the broken ground between shell holes. In the valley there was still a light smell of gas but not enough to worry us. The grass became long and the ground marshy, making the going difficult. At the bottom we came to a little brook. Our spool of wire was approaching the end and we saw that we would not have enough to reach the dugout on the other side which the fellows had picked out.

We, therefore, decided to cut the wire and ground it, taking the remaining wire to run a line from our present dugout to the rails, using the latter as a ground. We would then have our two stations in the same dugout and we could keep our party together for the night. In the morning we could rearrange our system for telephone communication.

We found an old steel corkscrew rod used in the construction of barbed wire barriers, and screwed it into the wet ground at the bottom of a shell hole. The four of us were grouped about the hole. Pete had the spool of wire, and Lens was watching me skin and scrape the wire to be fastened to the rod. Up to that moment the night had been quiet, too quiet entirely for comfort. The silence got on one's nerves; here we were right out by the entanglement on a front that has been one of the most active of the war and yet to all appearances there was not a living soul within miles of us.

A sudden flash of a "77" back of the German lines broke the spell. The report and whine of the approaching shell followed a second later. Our nerves were on edge for we all ducked, although the shell broke more than two hundred yards away. The explosion echoed up the valley. Then the silence closed down again, more penetrating than ever. Scotty reached up for the wire. I gave it to him and watched him make it fast. Then out of the darkness across the valley, a machine gun spoke:

"Rat—tat" (pause) "Rat—tat—tat"—(another pause).

Then another voice out forward answered "Rutta, rutta, rutta."

That was the beginning of the strangest conversation I ever heard, the machine gun outposts were talking to each other. I had heard the same thing on the Pexonne front several months earlier, but these fellows carried it further and seemed to enjoy it more. They repeated signals. They almost played tunes to each other, wasting much ammunition and not seeming to care a bit.

---

* Note: (Typed on Manuscript by Author) As a matter of fact this camouflaging game to hold the German divisions was being done on a grand scale. The landscape was being changed a little every night to fool enemy airmen into reporting new batteries which did not exist. There was even a story of fake wooden tanks and telegraph pole heavy guns.

The voice of the Boche is heavier, not so sharp; it is apt to be more regular than the Allies.

Here is a sample of the talk:

"Rat."

"Rutta."

"Rat, rat."

"Rutta, rutta."

"Rat, rat, rat."

"Rutta, rutta, rutta—rutta, rutta."

"Rat, rat; rat, rat, rat." (March time)

"Rutta rutta; rutta, rutta; rutta rutta rutta."

Here the American presses the button:

"R r r r r r r r r—."

The Boche might try to drown him out but more often he keeps silent until the flood is over, and then starts again more impudently than ever; "Rutta." That always means "Missed me, try again."[3]

The connection was made. We started back up the hill. Another shell came across, but we paid little attention; it was evident that they were not shooting at us. There was an observation post of some kind on our side of the valley. The Boche probably had gotten some idea of its location. Again silence closed down. I made the second connection; a ground on the rails. We reached the dugout without further incident. In the doorway, Schenck and Willman were waiting for us. This was their first experience with trench warfare and they were plainly relieved when they saw us coming.

The stove obstinately refused to do its duty, so we junked it, and ate cold "Corn Willie" and water. We set up one buzzer on the shelf at the entrance and the other on the end bunk. It was almost seven P.M. when we put across our first call. We decided Scotty would be XN and I X5; our call then was:

I calling,

KA XN de X5—CRV—AR.

Scotty answers,

KA X5 de XN—RTB—CRV—AR.

We called again at eight o'clock and thereafter every two hours throughout the night.

It was after eight, all lights were out. Willman was sitting up in the doorway keeping watch. The rest of us had rolled ourselves in our blankets on the dirty straw of the bunks (one learns not to be particular). I lay staring at the darkness and wondering at the uncanny stillness. We kept fully dressed with shoes on and gas masks for pillows. Willman's cigarette glowed brighter, a point of light in the absolute darkness. Presently there was a scurrying of little feet along the wall, followed by squealing in the corner. The rats were having a family quarrel, probably over our bread.

Then the "cooties" began to get busy. They were almost starved because the dugout had been empty for so long. They certainly were lively after they got started. Didn't really get going right until morning, and they stayed with us until we were sterilized back at Souilly. Willman was most afflicted; he couldn't even get rid of them by taking a bath and changing underwear. But more of "cooties" anon.

We went out at daybreak and took up our wire. Then we relayed it straight across the valley to an old position on the far side of the stream. We had talked over our first telephone conversation before we parted. Decided to make it just lineman's talk, as though we were putting in new "leads"; that, in itself, would interest the Germans. After that, every hour or so during the morning we talked and in between we sent our buzzer calls. We shifted the pitch of our instruments and used various calls to make it appear as though there were four or six stations operating.

Our conversations ran somewhat like this:

"Hello! Hello Buffalo!"

"Hello Scotty!"

"Hello! That you, Hank?"

"Yea. How you get me?"

"O.K. Where are you? Got it cut in yet?"

"Oh hell no! Only about half way."

"Better keep right after it. You know that's a rush order."

"We're moving right along, but we'll need more wire to cut 'er in."

"I'll send you down another spool right away. We got to get this job in this morning."

"I'll do my damndest, s'long."

Two hours later.

"Hello Buffalo! Hello!"

"Hello, Buffalo speaking."

"Hello, Scotty! Can you hear me?"

"Not very well. Speak louder."

"That's better. Have you got that line in yet?"

"No. I just got the new spool of wire a little while ago."

"Well, for Christ's sake, hurry up. That's supposed to be finished this morning. We got to get started on that cable this afternoon."

"All right, we'll get it done. Keep your shirt on. I'm only a little way from the board now."

"How much longer you think you'll be?"

"Oh! We'll have her cut in, in an hour or so."

"O.K. S'long."

"S'long."

About eight A.M. a Boche air scout came over. He flew recklessly low despite heavy shelling. He was followed by a second and a third. They stuck to it; kept coming back again and again even after several fights with some French Spads. These fellows were probably sent over to investigate increased activity. They were under direct orders because they took all kind of chances. Later, we were told that such enemy aerial activity was very unusual on that front.

About noon we put in a last conversation to the effect that the new lines were all in and everything was O.K.

Then we reeled in our wire; just pulled it across from one end without showing ourselves.

Chapter 11

Fort de Vaux

After the defeat of France in the war of 1870, General Sere de Rivière organized French frontier defenses by construction of a protective curtain of fortresses that stretched from north of Verdun to the city of Toul in the south. At first under separate commands, the autonomy of these forts was canceled in August 1915.[1] On February 21, 1916, the Germans, under the Crown Prince, launched extremely heavy attacks in the area of Verdun, with great carnage and loss of life on both sides. Many of the forts, hilltops and woods changed hands between the combatants many times. One of these was Fort Vaux which was about seven miles northeast of Verdun. My father's description of this fort coincides almost exactly with one that I recently heard from a member of an English flying club who flew over these forts in a light plane in the 1980s as part of a flying expedition from the British Isles. The damage to the outside has to be seen to be believed. The Germans used extremely heavy artillery preparation for their assaults.

In the quarry on the hill, the lieutenant and Holmes had set up their field wireless set. They began sending fake calls during the night and immediately were heavily shelled. The enemy direction finders had located them quickly and they were glad they had picked a sheltered spot in the quarry.

We proceeded along the heights east of Verdun toward the old concrete Fort de Vaux. It is hard to describe the condition of the ground here. It had been churned and kneaded by millions of shells during the great battle of Verdun two years before. The hills were ragged, barren clay with patches of stubble and weeds. To the east we could look down over enemy lines where fertile fields and patches of woods stretched away to the horizon. Several badly scarred villages could be seen in the distance.

As we approached the fort, its appearance astounded me. It resembled nothing so much as a prehistoric ruin. The entire outer surface of concrete had been ripped off to a depth of three to six feet, leaving the steel reinforcing rods sticking up all over it. The French estimated that at least a million shells had torn at it during the great assault.

We entered the place through a narrow passage from the bastion at the left forward corner. This bastion or outwork commanded the forward dry moat with a raking fire. The stone walls of the passageway were pitted and scarred from the shell splinters that had found their way in. We followed the narrow tunnel down two flights of steps and then through a very damp, dark cellar way at least fifty feet underground. There were long steps leading up and finally a doorway entering a small chapel. From the chapel another door opened into an arched hall crowded with men. Here we were under some thirty feet of concrete with practically no outside ventilation. The stuffy air weighed heavily on one's chest. A big acetylene searchlight blazed at either end of the hall. The mess tables had been shoved over against the left wall and the men were very boisterous and all in good humor. Door openings on the right led into sleeping quarters with bunks arranged all around the walls in tiers six feet high.

We ran our wire across between the two bastions in front of the fort. The German first line was just at the foot of the hill. A group of Frenchmen watched in silence. They could not understand our actions, and when we began working our buzzers, they became very suspicious.

"Non! Non! Ce n'est pas permis!" protested a little fellow. He became greatly excited and kept pulling the wire away and appealing to his friends, "Les Americans sont fou."

"Scotty and I did our best to explain but it was no use. He reported our doings to the Fort Commander. Of course we had presented our papers to the Major when we came into the fort and he had o.k.'d us. The French had to let us be but they could not get over the fact that we deliberately communicated with the enemy which in their eyes was treason.

Every two hours we sent our buzzer calls across the front of the fort. It began to get very cold and we nearly froze in the dampness of the outwork. Just before lights went out, we returned to the hall where we found all of the bunks occupied. There was no room in the sleeping quarters, so we spread out our blankets on the mess tables. Willman made his bed on two benches close to the wall. A fire hose dropped over his bunk from a bracket at the end of the hall.

We had settled ourselves for a good night, when a huge rat came galloping up the hose. The rodent was as big as a cat, and the hose shook under its weight. A shower of dust fell on Willman's face. He sat up and swore, scaring the rat so badly that it all but fell off the hose. It scampered to the socket in the wall, turned in desperation and made a whirlwind dash back down the swaying hose. Willman let out a whoop and struck wildly at it. Too late, a flying leap and the beast was gone, lost in the rubbish and piping in the corner.

We again settled ourselves. Slowly the incident faded from my mind. I was wandering off into happy dreams of peace and home when a wild sputtering and gurgling on the benches beside me brought me back. Willman was sitting up, wiping his face on his arm and spitting when he could spare time between oaths. "The damn—ftoo ee —beast ran right over my face," he complained. "Stuck its b——, b——ff foot in my mouth—ftoo ee."

"Ah why in hell don't you keep your mouth shut then," suggested Shenk, rolling over sleepily. "For Christ's sake, cut out the row and let a fellow get to sleep."

Willman grumbled something about a cruel world, pulled the cover over his head, and presently was sawing wood louder than ever.

When I opened my eyes again, the lights at the end of the hall were on. Men were talking. It was morning; after six by my watch, but of course not a ray of daylight came down to us. We went outside. Coming into the open air was like throwing a weight off one's chest. Breathing deeply to get the stagnant air out of my lungs made me giddy.

We got away with coffee at the French kitchen by a sad tale of hard luck and then hotcakes at the doughboy's mess.

We sent a few more calls during the morning and then tramped back to the quarry where Holmes and Lens had been operating the spark set to the bewilderment of Fritz. The truck was to meet us there at four o'clock to take us back to Souilly. We waited until almost five, spending the time to very good purpose: cootie hunting. Willman held the record; he picked them off by twos and threes and soon lost count. Scotty was feeling very good, he acted as though he had tasted champagne that morning. No doubt the French in the bastion of the fort where he and Peterson had spent the night had been good to him.

Several Boche planes came over and we watched the work of the antiaircraft batteries. The city of Verdun lay in a haze in the distance, with the sun setting gloriously over it. Beautiful purple and rose tints spread over the landscape as the red ball of fire sunk into the mist. We all remarked upon the peculiar light effect. To me it was a symbol of the end of the war. The blood of the thousands who had died here seemed to ooze out of the ground in the fading light and to be sucked up through the haze to the clouds and the sun.[2]

"On ne passe pas" had meant the death of hundreds of thousands but Verdun had held. Now the tide has definitely turned and the end is a matter of days. The Germans have asked for an armistice and negotiations are under way to end it. Our intercept stations here at Souilly have gotten the message direct from Berlin. They are asking for permission to take enough food with them to feed their armies on the way home.

November 1st.

The drive started again to the north this morning. The bombardment had been very heavy in that direction since before daylight. Over three hundred aeroplanes have flown over here. We counted as many as ninety-three in the air at one time. Man certainly has made the birds look like amateurs. They are all going over to bomb the German lines of communication. I would not like to be in Sedan today.

There is nothing doing to the east of the Meuse and I'll bet this is puzzling the Boche. There are many wireless reports of peace negotiations. It looks like the old war is on its last legs.

November 3rd.

The First Army has advanced over fifteen miles. They have gone right through and are approaching Stenay and Beaumont. Long range guns are bombarding Sedan which is on the German main line of supplies.

November 12th.

"Ray! Guerre finish!" was the way the French hailed us when the news came out. We received the wireless dispatch of the German acceptance of the Allied armistice terms at nineteen o'clock (7 P.M.) on November 10th. The French simply went wild. They ran around like crazy, shouting at the top of their lungs and beating tin pans. There were many "Pinard" and Champagne parties of course and we could hear them singing and laughing until late that night.

Chapter 12

Armistice

Today, in the 1990s, the vast majority of World War I veterans are no longer with us. Those of us who served in World War II remember a rather different kind of war termination than that described in this chapter. Pockets of resistance, particularly in the Pacific arena, remained for a considerable time after the war's formal end, and the Army warned us about going into certain areas alone. Of the items described in this final chapter, I remember particularly well the fleece-lined vest, which I believe my mother disposed of, because of its ratty condition, when we moved around 1938. Our family still has several items obtained from German prisoners including helmets, binoculars, a Luger automatic and the field telephone shown in the photographs in this book.

On the morning of November 11, I awoke at six o'clock and couldn't but feel disappointed at the sound that greeted me. The barrage certainly did not sound like the war was over; every gun on the front seemed to be firing as fast as it could.

Rosen on the bunk opposite me was slipping into his shoes and winding his puttees.

"They're using up surplus ammunition this morning," he remarked with a yawn. He had been to the French party and gotten to bed at two A.M. "The French got word this morning that it'll be all over at eleven A.M. I'm going up and see the finish. Nothing doing around here."

He was already strapping on his pistol belt and reaching for his tin hat. His unbounded nervous energy would not let him be still. If there were anything going on, Rosen had to be there. But this idea of his intrigued me. It was a stupendous event; a day of days in history.

"Wait a minute, Rosen," I said. "I'm coming along."

"Atta boy, Sarge. I'll meet you down at the kitchen. Kind of chilly this morning. Mighty glad they issued these vests the other day. Damn near as warm as overcoats and much more comfortable."

The vests he referred to are special equipment; heavy fleece-lined leather worn over the service coat and extending well down the thigh. They shed rain and keep the body warm without encumbering the arms and legs.

We hit the highway toward Verdun. The thunder of heavy bombardment was continuous all the way from northwest to southeast. The U.S. Second Army south of Verdun had started the drive toward Briey and Metz and the rumble of the guns was even heavier in that direction than to the north.

We soon hopped a truck which took us right into Verdun. We held First Army sector passes which would see us through all sentries and anyway this was a holiday and everybody was in a good humor. We chose the region east of Verdun because it was nearest, and here the lines were still stationary and definitely defined.

We visited the wireless station again and the boys were delighted to see us. They were celebrating with a couple of bottles of wine and the cook had some breakfast left.

Regularly, every two or three minutes, a long range shell came whistling over and cracked near the barracks or railroad yards. This shelling had been continuous since 1916. The men at the station paid no attention whatever. They had been there three months and to them the explosives were part of the place. They would miss them when they stopped.

* * * * * * * * * * * * * * * * * *

We entered the front lines a little before eleven A.M. There were very few troops in the close-up positions. A platoon of infantry lay at rest in the lee of a hill and we came upon a group of French artillerymen seated on boxes around a fire. They waved Pinard bottles and shouted: "Vive Les Americans! Guerre finish! Boche Caput!"

Presently we joined a machine gun squad in a little hollow on the edge of a wood. They pointed across rough open country to a thin strip of wire and some freshly turned earth several hundred yards off.

It was almost eleven o'clock and the guns were delivering themselves of a last blast of fury. The machine gunners were quarreling, good-naturedly enough, over the privilege of holding the trigger down during the last minute.

And then suddenly, magically, the bombardment died. There were a few more heavy detonations to the south and then an almost unbelievable silence. A moment later, when the realization sank in, one gunner grabbed the other and they did a rough and tumble dance of glee, laughing and shouting. Everybody threw their tin hats in the air and of course some fell out in the open with the result that soon we were all out.

They wanted to go across but had orders not to move. No such orders held us. Over there, as we started through the stubby fields, we could see grey clad figures moving about.

Some half dozen Germans stood watching us thread our way through the wire and approach their trench. It gave us a creepy feeling to be thus meeting the enemy in the open on the parapet of his own trench.

These Germans did not smile; they eyed us solemnly and spoke to each other in undertones. Presently they were crowding around us and others came running up to join the throng. We were curiosities in their eyes and strangely enough their interest centered in our fleece-lined vests. When they found that we could speak German, they became friendly and offered us their pistols, helmets and even watches as souvenirs in exchange for our vests. Their eagerness for the vests became so great that we began to fear that they might take them from us by force. Then a young kid came up and pushed through the crowd.

"Wenn Sie so gut sein wollen," he began very politely. "Der Herr Leutnant möchte mit Ihnen sprechen." It was an invitation to speak to the officer.

We followed the orderly down a flight of steps.

"Die Amerikaner, Herr Leutnant." He introduced us.

The officer was standing at the end of the dugout with his hands behind his back. He tried to look very dignified and soldierly but the chief impression I got was one of extreme youth. He was certainly not over twenty, adolescently slender, smooth pink face and close cropped hair brushed up to stand on end.

"We are pleased to become acquainted with worthy antagonists," he said in German. "I am told you speak German. I hope my people have not molested you."

We assured him they had not and then he began to ply us with questions about America. What part of the country we came from and what it was like. He appeared to be deeply interested in everything American. He expressed wonder at the size of our Colt .45's and great admiration for our fleece-lined vests. He gave me the impression that the first chance he got he was coming to the States.

"Wenn der Handel nur wieder kommt,"[1] he said thoughtfully.

I agreed with him that the free interchange of trade was the one thing that would heal the wounds of the war and reminded him that was what we were in the war for.

He just waved his hand and smiled. "Der Krieg ist zu Ende. Wer noch da ist geht jetzt heim."

THE END

EPILOGUE

America found herself with over a million troops in Europe after the Armistice on November 11. Gradually the flood of men and supplies to France was slowed down. There still remained the problem of what to do with all the troops overseas. Some, of course, were used for the army of occupation of Germany, while others were used to aid the White Russians against the Communists. Fear of bolshevism appears in military records as early as 1919. Some contain comments such as "these men show no tendency toward bolshevism."

One solution was the creation of an A.E.F. University in southern France where soldiers could attend classes and be trained for civilian life while awaiting orders to be shipped home through the port of Marseilles. My father's manuscript ends with the Armistice, but his notes tell of the same type of letdown and confusion as occurred after World War II. There is mention of an incident on December 30, 1918 where a Lt. Nelson tried to make him become a truck driver and my father objected, saying that he didn't know how and that that was not his specialty, or MOS as we called it in World War II. This irritated the lieutenant and he threatened to have my father busted. Dad discovered that the officer had been a corporal in the regular Army for seventeen years and that he had served in Mexico against Pancho Villa. He also discovered that field promotions could not be taken away in this manner, since my father had been promoted to sergeant on merit and not merely to fill a slot. Lt. Nelson was thwarted. However, Sergeant Hinrichs did drive a Ford touring car from Dijon to Langres on January 7, 1919 and apparently did a little partying on the way. Later he drove to Neufchâteau. Equipment was being returned to the units of ownership.

From messages on old postcards (See Appendix C), we know that by February 8 Hinrichs was nicely ensconced in a hilltop hotel at Menton, France, on the Côte d'Azur, and that he took a short walk over the border to Italy. By March 15 he had passed through Chaumont on his way to enrollment at the A.E.F. University at Beaune.

From personal communication I know that my father did go to Germany after the war was over, though probably only on leave. He spoke with some members of our family, because at one point he mentioned to me some of their reaction to being occupied by units of French Colonial Forces. It was not favorable. Such feelings were the crucible of the 1940 Vichy Armistice. In war, action equals reaction. As I write this in the spring of 1993, the Serbs have been attacking the Bosnians in reaction to the Battle of Kosovo in 1389, with Sarajevo under siege. Concomitantly, the Croats and the Moslems have been carrying out their own atrocities. And now, just as the West

This photo of my father was taken somewhere in southern France early in 1919. Note the flowers over the medals.

Germans were our very essential allies in the Cold War, we will join with our former enemies, the Russians, to try to stabilize the area. There is some merit to the contention of the Quakers that war never really settles anything. Old, bald headed DI's may not like this, but it is true. After all, it was in Sarajevo that the flames of World War I were first ignited.

By July, 1919 my father was back in the U.S.A. He went up to our summer home in Pennsylvania. That same summer he was badly injured in the foot while clearing brush on a neighbor's property and had to spend most of the summer on crutches. He recovered completely, but the incident shows that the hand of fate is uncontrollable in both peace and in war. For a while my father worked as a Packard truck salesman and ran the Cable Code business at night, but the postwar depression soon ended both jobs. After he met my mother, he started dental school at the University of Maryland in the fall of 1921, taking this course because it was suggested by his future father-in-law, Dr. Ryland O. Sadler, of Baltimore. He graduated in 1925 and opened a dental office with a four thousand dollar loan. Today, the dollar amount required to start a dental practice would probably be twenty-five times as much.

The reason I have emphasized the aviation aspects in the text is that his interest in this subject became apparent to me at an early age. I can remember going with him to watch Curtiss Jennies take off from an early airport north of Baltimore at Park Heights Avenue and Old Court Road near Druid Ridge Cemetery and slightly later going to Baltimore's old Logan Field, opposite what is now the Dundalk Marine Terminal. Here planes were slightly newer, like the Lockheed Vega, later used by Amelia Earhart and Wiley Post. It is frustrating that the only plane he called by name in the text was the Spad. In the early thirties he bought me a pack of six solid model kits through an advertisement in *Parents* Magazine. He meticulously constructed the balsa wood model of Baron Manfred von Richtofen's Red Fokker Dr. I triplane. Sometimes, he would cast small airplane parts for me from base metal in his dental office. He would talk about the gaudy colors of von Richtofen's flying circus and was an admirer of Ernst Udet, a surviving German Ace who would come to America from time to time. Until they were removed, he would complain about the aviation restrictions of the Versailles Treaty, and he spoke of how the Germans were catapulting planes from ships to accomplish early delivery of mail on the North Atlantic run. His interest in the air was a general thing, and included all nations. In later years we would all go out to Curtis-Wright Airport on Smith Avenue, which was near our home in Mount Washington. It was here that I was taken on my first airplane flight, in a Travel-Air monoplane,

Inspection before entraining. Beaune, June, 1919.

in 1933. Other passengers on that flight were three Chinese who were being trained at the field for Chiang Kai-shek—a foreshadowing of things to come.

Slightly later, in the middle thirties, the *Emden*, a "pocket battleship" built under Versailles Treaty restrictions, came to Baltimore, and my father took me down on a visit. It is odd, but my memory of the British Cruiser *Exeter*, which I visited in 1937, is much clearer to me than that of the *Emden*. It gave me a thrill to sneak my camera aboard the British ship and photograph the Supermarine Walrus amphibian. I still have the photos. I do remember clearly being taken to a soccer game between the *Emden* crew and a local team at Gwynn Oak Park. The ship's team lost by a large score, but I well remember the music at the end, with the entire team giving the Nazi salute—another foreshadowing. My father said that the Germans lost because they were unable to practice while at sea. It was somewhat after this that Hitler reoccupied the Rhineland. My father approved.

It was in this period that he began giving the talks to the North Baltimore Lions Club that I mentioned in the foreword. As one crisis followed another in the late thirties, our family became true news junkies. Periodically crises would occur in Europe, usually on weekends. Then America began to split apart because of the America First movement. Colonel Charles Lindberg took the isolationist position, and we all admired him. I remember going to the Lyric theater in Baltimore to hear Marine Corps General Smedley Butler speak against American entry into World War II. The theater was full. It was because of his attitude about American expeditions into Nicaragua in the twenties and thirties that this Major General never became Commandant of the Marine Corps. He offended the politicos in the Marine Officer Corps. His theme was that for the average volunteer it was "Hello, Sucker!"

In particular, my father was quite resentful of the fact that the only country that had repaid its war debt to the U.S. was little Finland. He felt that the main reason that the U.S. had entered World War I was to rescue the Morgan financial empire, which had underwritten war bonds of the British and French governments and was heavily involved in lending money to them for armaments purchases.[1] Having lost much money in the 1914 bankruptcy

Boxcar loaded with troops on the way to Port of Embarkation in France. That the car is American can be determined by the four wheel American style arch bar trucks and by the words "Wagon Americain" stenciled on the side.

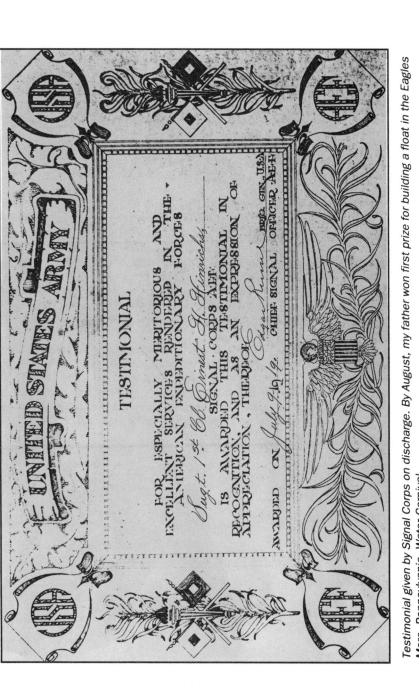

Testimonial given by Signal Corps on discharge. By August, my father won first prize for building a float in the Eagles Mere, Pennsylvania, Water Carnival.

of the New Haven Railroad and other ventures, for J. P. Morgan it was a fact that it was imperative that the Allies win World War I. Financing the loans to the Allied Powers would have been impossible without the creation of the Federal Reserve Board in 1913. We often heard of "British Propaganda," and there is no doubt in my mind that it did exist. In 1939 or 1940 my father bought a powerful short wave radio so he could listen to DNB, the German North American Broadcasting Service. I now understand the reasons for this action more completely since working on this manuscript. Dad's argument was, "Why should we pull the English chestnuts out of the fire a second time?"

On September 3, 1939 my father appeared in my bedroom in the early hours of the morning to tell me that war had started again. He hugged me. "Quelle guerre! Quelle Stupidité!" He didn't actually say that, but he probably thought it. I was seventeen.

It is likely that these emotional conflicts of my father caused him to suggest that I stay with the troops when the ASTP program for training dentists was terminated by the Army in the summer of 1944. So I left dental school while in good academic standing and took basic training at Camp Barkley, Texas, now Dyess Airforce Base. I didn't know it at the time, but I was starting a secondary military career, arriving off Leyte on September 2, 1945. Then, with the war over, my father wanted me to get home and go back to school. Of course, I was perfectly aware that there were thousands of men who deserved to go home ahead of me, which was only fair. I pointed this out to him by mail but was back in civilian life by April, 1946, graduating from dental school in 1948.

With all the present day immigrants to America, legal and illegal, my father's ethnic problems will seem minuscule compared to what could occur in the future. Our treatment of our Japanese citizens in World War II has come back to haunt us. I do remember, however, that as the Chinese crossed the Yalu River and trapped American troops at the Chosin Reservoir, my father spoke sympathetically of a Chinese patient who came into his office and was apologizing for what had happened. Dad was empathic, having been in a similar position.

Ernest H. Hinrichs, Jr.

APPENDIX A

Receipt Signed by Corporal Hinrichs for Service Records of Men in His Squad.

For those training to be Listening Post operators, some of the tactical work was replaced by training in Morse code and telegraphy and intensive study of military German. My father had been promoted to corporal while at Fort Meade in the 313th Infantry. There was a marked shortage of competent German-speaking radio operators. The following receipt, written in longhand, was found in the National Archives:

Army Signal Schools
U. S. A. P. O. 714
3 May 1918

Rec'd this date Service records
of the following men.
Corp Ernest H. Henrichs
Corp Keller, John P.
Corp Israel, Mortimer J.
Corp Shuster, George N.
Pvt 1Cl Holmes, Ray H.
Pvt 1Cl Kaplan, Louis A.
Pvt Beaman, Snowden P.
Pvt Greubel, William G.

(signed) Ernest H. Hinrichs
Cpl
In charge

Left 3 May 1918 per Par 19 SO 121
G Hq AEF [sic] 1918

The only part of this receipt that was in my father's handwriting was his rank and signature and the words "in charge." The spelling of the name Hinrichs is even worse in some of the Army's typed orders. They seem to have had as much trouble in 1918 as in 1944 and 1953. I think that the problem has become much less prevalent since the computer appeared on the scene.

See Record Group 120, Entry 401, Box 1785, File 201.1 and Box 1786, File 220.3, National Archives, Washington, D.C.

Army Signal School
U.S.A. P.O. 714
3 May 1918

Rec'd this date Service records
of the following Men.

Corp Ernest H Heinrichs
Corp Keller, John P
Corp Israel Martiner J
Corp Shuster George N
Pvt 1Cl Holmes Ray H
Pvt 1Cl Kaplan Louis A
Pvt Beaman Snowden P
Pvt Greubel William G

                    Ernest H Heinrichs
                              Cpl

                         In charge

Sept 3 May 1918 per Par 19 SO 121.
S Hq AE 7 1918

APPENDIX B

Letter Questioning the Loyalty of William Gerard Greubel and Other Men Born in Germany. Letter Stressing the Need for German-Speaking Radio Operators.

A visit to the National Archives confirmed what I had long suspected, namely that my father had changed the name of the Treubel character from something else. He undoubtedly did this because at the time he was writing in the 1930's it was quite likely that Treubel was alive. There is pretty good evidence that the things my father says about him were true and also that the brass had suspicions about him before he was grilled and removed from the front on June 3rd. The names of most of the men mentioned in my father's text can be found in various rosters and letters at the Signal School, but nowhere is there anyone named Treubel. If you change only the first letter of the name in the following communication you can see what happened:

ARMY SIGNAL SCHOOLS
AMERICAN EXPEDITIONARY FORCES
FRANCE

May 10th, 1918.

From   : Commandant, Army Signal Schools, American E. F.
To   : Commanding General, American E. F., A. P. O. 706.
Subject : Soldier born in Germany—Radio Intelligence Service.

    1. Attention is invited to the fact that William Gerard Greubel reported at this school on April 9th, 1918, for instruction in Radio Intelligence work, and was relieved on May 3rd per Par 19, SO 121, GHQ, AEF, C.S. for duty with the 42nd Division on Radio Intelligence work "listening in." The records of this office show that this soldier was born in Germany.

    2. In this connection it is deemed pertinent to state that there are no records here available showing the place of birth of other men who have passed through these schools and been assigned to the Radio Intelligence section for "listening in" service.

3. In view of the peculiar nature of the work, it is believed that the reliability and loyalty of every man of German birth, employed in the Radio Intelligence service, should be thoroughly known.

Carl F. Hartman

CFH/MI   Colonel, Signal Corps, U.S.A.

R. G. 120, E. 401, Box 1783, File 201.1 also E. 403, N. A. Washington, D.C.

That the A.E.F. was having difficulty obtaining a sufficient number of German-speaking radio operators is quite evident from the following communication:

General Headquarters
AMERICAN EXPEDITIONARY FORCES
Second Section, G. S.

July 7, 1918

From: Asst.   Chief of Staff, G-2, G.H.Q., A.E.F.

To: Commandant, Army Schools, A.E.F.

Subject: German-Speaking Operators for Listening-in Stations.

1. Referring to communication from Commandant, Army Signal Schools, A.E.F., transmitted by your first endorsement, file 221.35, you are advised that unless there is positive evidence that the soldiers mentioned, who are native born citizens of the U.S., are in any way disloyal to the U.S., no steps will be taken to relieve them, in view of the difficulty to secure German-speaking soldiers.

2. As regards Corporal H. E. Kahl and Private 1st Class G. L. Potgeter, who were born in Germany, steps have been taken now to investigate their past history.

By direction:

A. Moreno
Major, General Staff, A.E.F.

AM
ejk

221.35 (HAS)   1st Ind.   JR/c

HQ. ARMY SCHOOLS, American E. F., France, July 8, 1918 – To Director, Army Signal School, American E. F.

R. G. 120, E. 401, Box 1789, file 352. N. A., Washington, D.C.

APPENDIX C

Pre- and Post-World War I Postcard Messages

A number of prewar and postwar postcards survive with messages of historical interest. The dates given are either postmark dates or were written on the card by my father.

Sept. 3, 1908. Mailed from Frankfurt with a picture of Giessen, where the G. W. Gail tobacco factory was located. Card is addressed to Mr. John Hinrichs Jr. Pension Metropole, Frankfurt. Bockenheimer Land Str. Message says: "Dear Johnny, This is a dinky little place and seems full of aunts and uncles. We leave tomorrow for Rotterdam. It is cold here and cloudy. Love to Paul and Dad. From your brother, Ink." My father would never reveal how he got the nickname of "Ink," even to his own children.

Feb. 8, 1919. Military cancellation and mailed to his mother. Message says: "This is our Hotel. Everything is paid for by the Government. The food is excellent. I am in a room with two other fellows, a Sgt. and a Cpl. Very congenial. Individual beds and A1 service. This picture gives you no idea of the beauty of the place. Ink." The brightly colored card shows the funicular railway in Menton going up the mountain to the hotels.

Feb. 8, 1919. Italian cancellation with postage stamp and mailed to his mother. "In Italy, just walked over the border. Menton is less than five kilometers from the line. The 'Côte d'Azur' is certainly the garden spot of Europe. There is some truth in 'sunny France' after all. Ink." An Italian card with a photo of Bordighera.

Feb. 14, 1919. A card mailed to: Sgt. 1st Cl. E. H. Hinrichs at 12th Service Co., A. P. O. #731 A.E.F. and passed by military censor from Neves, Germany, with an illustration of the amphitheater at Trier. Message says: "Dear Friend, I received your nice letter the other day and am glad to hear that you are O.K. and that you are going on furlough. I sure hope you have a nice time and would like to go with you. I am going to try to go up to Coblenz and take a peep at the Rhine before I go back. I have a good place here and hope I stay until I go home which I of course hope will happen soon. Best regards. Hoping to hear from you soon. Ralph E. Lenz, c/o Post Signal Office, A.P.O. 930, Neves, Germany. A.E.F."

No date or cancellation, addressed to his mother, and probably enclosed in a letter. "Passed through here on my way to Beaune. Am now enrolled at the schools. Address mail as follows: A.E.F. University, A.P.O. 909, Beaune, Cote d'Or, France. Will write soon. Ink." Shows a picture of Chaumont—L'Hotel de Ville.

February 17, 1919. No date or cancellation, and probably enclosed in a letter to his mother. "At Chalon this afternoon, Saturday 17th. Lorentz and I took passes to Lyon and got off the train here. Lyon is about five hours further and wouldn't arrive before midnight. Shall probably stay here. Chalon is not a very big place and there is nothing much to see. Ink" Card shows Obelisk street in Chalon-Sur-Saone.

March 15, 1919. Card has no address and was probably enclosed in a letter. "Dear Ma, Am enclosing the 'Menu' of Beaune University. You can take anything from A to Z (Astronomy to Zoology). At least you can on paper. I have marked the courses I have elected; only three are permitted. Looks like the place may be all right after she gets started. Rather a mix up at present. Let us hope there will be an improvement in mess; at present it is an awful come down [*sic*] from the 12th Service Co. feed. Reveille at 6 A.M. No chance to get lazy. Ink." Card shows a picture of Beaune Hospice.

April 19, 1919. "This is a very interesting old building, Municipal hospital and museum combined. Went through the place several weeks ago. E.H.H." Also shows Beaune Hospice.

No date, cancellation, or address. "This cathedral was built after the city was spared during the Franco-Prussian war. It is not yet finished. Much of the carving is incomplete as can be seen in the exterior view." Picture is a photo of the interior of Lyon cathedral.

APPENDIX D

Note on the High Power T.P.S. Used With a Rotary Converter or Alternator

The T. M. buzzers are not sufficient to obtain an alternating current of 300 to 1200 periods of some importance (say over 100 watts); it is possible, indeed, to connect several buzzers in parallel as it has already been tried, but they must have a same period and it is not practical to connect more than two buzzers in parallel in the same circuit.

Rotary converters or alternators can then be used.

Rotary converters may be constructed for any power, for some hundred watts as well as for several Kilowatts; they need a source of continuous current of a corresponding power; if this current is provided by accumulators, their weight becomes very considerable when more than a few hundred watts are needed. All depends of course on the length of time during which such a power is used; if it is for short and infrequent signals, a battery may be worked at a high rate (as for starting motor cars), say 400 or 500 watts for a 28 Kgs. battery (two 10 volt—20 ampere-hour batteries), whereas for long telegraph messages, the same 28 Kilograms battery could only give 100 to 150 watts.

Whenever the power will exceed 500 watts, it will generally be more practical to use a small electric set such as a light gasoline motor and alternator, than heavy and clumsy batteries inasmuch as the charging of the latter would anyhow require the use, behind the lines, of an electric set at least as heavy as the other one. In many cases, however, it may be advisable to use rotary converters with accumulators.

They are practical for T.P.S. only when the power varies between 100 and 500 watts. For this purpose, two types of portable rotary converters have been built and tested by the "Télégraphie Militaire," the T M No. 1 and the T M No. 2.

It is unnecessary to give any information concerning the use of alternators for T.P.S., as they are worked very easily.

IMPORTANT NOTICE: The conditions surrounding the installation of the high power T.P.S. are usually more favorable than those surrounding that of the portable stations in the lst lines; one will thus dispose of about ten minutes to set the station up. The

117

connections with the earth should therefore be made very carefully, with as small a resistance as possible (line), so as to turn to good account as much of the power as possible.

ARMY SIGNAL SCHOOLS
AMERICAN EXPEDITIONARY FORCES
FRANCE

TÉLÉGRAPHIE PAR SOL (T.P.S.)

Télégraphie par Sol means literally "telegraphy through the ground." Oscillations much lower in frequency than radio oscillations are set up in the ground and carried to a distant point where they are received. The number of oscillations used in T.P.S. are only a few hundred per second, which is within the limits of audio frequency.

The two terminals of the secondary of an induction coil are buried in the ground, and the current passes from one of these bases to the other. This of course sets up electrostatic and electromagnetic lines of force in the earth—these being reversed once during every cycle. Both travel to the receiving station. Tests have shown that it is the electromagnetic lines that are best carried by the earth. Therefore, it is the inductive effect that affects the receiver more than the difference of potential at its bases. That has been described in a previous lecture (Listening-In) about the effect of the different kinds of soil, etc., and is true in T.P.S. also.

The range varies. Three kilometers is the normal range. Increasing the distance between the two bases, either at the receiving or sending stations, increases the range. The greatest range is obtained when the line connecting the two bases at the receiving station is parallel to the line connecting the two bases at the transmitting station. The stations must be directly opposite from each other. This arrangement is shown in **Figure I.**

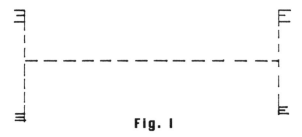

Fig. I

If this arrangement is impossible, the next best thing is to have the line joining the two stations make equal angles with each base line as shown in **Figure II.**

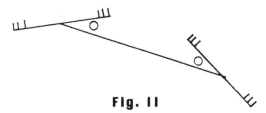

Fig. II

The minimum distance between the base lines is 50 meters. The bases should make good contact with the ground. If a large piece of metal or metal screening is not available, 5 or 6 metal pickets should be used, and the ground dampened where they are driven. The wire leading to the bases must be well insulated, a metal-covered cable such as lead cable should never be used. It is not necessary that the wire be straightened between the bases, i.e., it may turn corners if necessary.

The transmitting set consists of a Buzzer (T. M. No. 2, No. 2-bis, No. 2-ter). The electrical circuit of the buzzer is shown in **Figure III.**

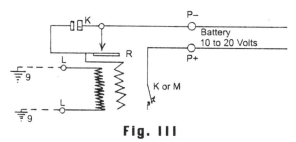

Fig. III

The primary current is supplied by a 10 or 20 volt battery giving 2 to 3 amperes. The resultant current in the secondary circuit varies with the resistance of the ground. It is from $1/4$ to 1 ampere. The resistance of the ground is about 100 ohms. The terminals of the primary circuit are marked (+) and (-), and this polarity should be observed. In the No. 2-bis and No. 2-ter sets, weights are furnished to load the vibrator so as to vary its time and hence the frequency of the secondary output. In each buzzer there is what is called a critical frequency. This is the frequency at which the secondary circuit and the primary circuit are in resonance. The radiated energy is then very small. Hence this frequency should be avoided. The critical frequency is usually marked on the box. The receiving sets consist of two bases and an amplifier in series with them. The 3-ter amplifier is usually used. The same precautions about the bases should be observed at the station as at the transmitting station. Increasing the distance between the bases increases the sensitiveness of receiving. In practice, this distance can usually be made large.

Damp soil is not favorable for the use of the T.P.S. The reason is that the ground circuit between the transmitting bases has very little resistance, hence there is not much radiation. Electrical circuits and strays in the ground, such as would come from power stations, grounded wires, and a central telephone station, interfere with the use of the T.P.S. The following circuit will cut out strays to a great extent.

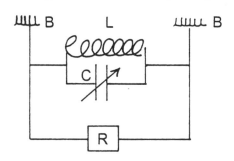

Tune the circuit LC to the frequency you wish to receive. When so tuned, this offers a very high resistance to waves of that frequency—hence they pass to the receiver R. Waves of other frequencies oscillate in the LC circuit and hence dissipate their energy there.

To avoid interference from other T.P.S. sets, besides using the circuit just explained, the sets may be orientated as explained in connection with Fig. I and Fig. II. Also, the interfering sets may be assigned different frequencies, and an operator soon learns to distinguish signals of his own pitch from those of different pitch.

APPENDIX E

Report on French Listening Stations

Not to be Taken Into Front Line Trenches

O.C.S.O., A.E.F.

June 18, 1918

1. The information contained in this report was obtained at a T.P.S. conference of French Officers held at Plessis Belleville, February 28–March 1, 1918. The French officers attending the conference were each in charge of T.P.S. and listening station work at the French front.

INTRODUCTORY

2. The report consists of two main parts: Part 1, which gives the method of organization of a listening station as now used in the French Army, and Part 2, which gives a description of apparatus and experimental details. In Part 2 are also taken up some of the various difficulties which a listening station may encounter and some methods of overcoming these difficulties. A number of cases actually met in the field are used to illustrate the various points. The information given in Part 2 is of particular value, because it is the result of three years of practical experiments of French officers at the front.

PART I

3. The French Organization of a Listening Station.

(a) Personnel. The personnel of a listening station consists of twelve men, as follows:

1 Sergeant, who is chief of station. He is an "interprete"—i.e., he can read Morse code, and has knowledge of the German language.

2 Corporals, who are also interpretes. One of these is second in command of the station.

3 Interpretes.

121

4 Wiremen or mechanics. These men are not necessarily interpretes, but it is desirable that they should be. Their duties are to test and repair the lines, apparatus, take care of storage batteries, etc.

4. <u>Question</u>. Is an expert operator, i.e., one who can read Morse code, but who has no knowledge of German, likely to be a useful man in a listening station? <u>Answer</u>. Yes. Because a large part of the signals intercepted are signals in Morse code from the T.P.S. sets of the enemy. The interception of telephone conversation is not such a frequent occurrence, although much conversation has been overheard, particularly in the earlier years of the war.

5. <u>Question</u>. Where do the French get their men for interpretes? <u>Answer</u>. It has been the custom to take men from the border provinces, such as Alsace and Lorraine, who already have a knowledge of German, and teach them the Morse code.

6. (b) <u>Relief of Station</u>. Each station of twelve men is on continuous duty for ten days. At the expiration of this period, it is relieved and allowed a ten-day rest. During the time of rest, the men are given any special training necessary, and other light duties. These duties consist in large part in putting in order apparatus, charging the accumulators, etc.

7. At the station only one man, who is necessarily an interprete, listens at a time. Thus, three interpretes could take care of a twenty-four hour day by working in three 8-hour shifts. The French usually try to limit to two hours the length of time a single observer is on duty; it sometimes happens, however, that a man be kept for four hours; it was found that a man could not do efficient work if kept on duty longer than four hours.

8. In addition to the regular personnel of the stations, there are some extra wiremen, or mechanics, about four for each four stations. These men stay either at the base station (see paragraph 9), or at the station where extra apparatus is kept and the accumulators are charged. Usually the base station and this station are in the same place.

9. (c) <u>Staff Organization and Reports</u>. Each listening station is connected by special wires (telegraph or telephone) to the base station, which is some distance back of the lines. To this base station also come communication wires from a sound-observation post and a visual-observation post.
    The personnel of the base station consists of eight men, as follows:

> 1 Officer, Lieutenant or Sous-Lieutenant who is chief of post.
> 2 Sous-Officers, either adjutants or sergeants.
> 2 Sergeants who are interpretes.
> 2 Privates.
> 1 Clerk.

10. The officer who is chief of station reports to the chief of the intelligence service of the War Department.
    In a given sector, there may be four listening stations, each of which is connected to the base station, shown diagrammatically in **Figure 1**. In addition, each listening station is connected by direct wire communications to the Chef de Batallion or to the Colonel of the infantry regiment.

11. The chief of a listening station makes a daily report of everything that has been heard during the last 24 hours, with a translation of the German conversation. One copy is sent to the Etat Major de L'Armee (télégraphie et 2nd Bureau) (the 2nd Bureau is the Intelligence Service of the War Department); one copy to the 2nd Bureau Corps d'Armee; and one copy to the 2nd Bureau Division. This last copy is read by the Colonel of the regiment of infantry.

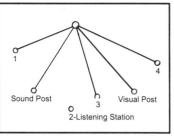

Fig. 1

12. Cipher messages are taken down exactly as they come, and are sent directly to the Cipher Bureau of the Army.

PART II

13. Apparatus and Experimental Details.
There are two general types of collecting wires, or antennae. The first type consists of a large loop insulated from the ground. The second type consists of a long insulated wire with its terminals connected to earth. We will describe each type in detail.

14. The loop is approximately a rectangle from 300 to 1,200 m. in length and from 150 to 500 m. in width. Either one, two, three, and sometimes four, twins in series are used. The actual shape and size of the loop is largely dependent upon external conditions, such as contour of trenches, nearness to the enemy's lines, etc. The loop is laid out with its long side parallel to the enemy's lines, and the side of the loop nearest the enemy is usually placed in the first line French trench. The wire must be protected from shell fire, and hence it is absolutely necessary to place it in a region of protection, such as a trench. Occasionally natural objects, such as a river, may be made use of (see problem discussed in paragraph 25). The loop must be well insulated. The resistance between loop and ground should be 60,000 ohms or more. The wire of the loop is supported on insulators, preferably porcelain, sometimes wooden, which are attached to wooden stakes, about a meter in length, which are driven in the bottom of the trench. The wire is fastened to the insulating supports by tie-strings, and sometimes by pieces of wire, although strings were considered better. Metal staples should never be used for the purpose of fastening the wire to the stakes, for this method is liable to cause breaks in the insulation. If the wire of the loop has to cross the trench, it is brought across overhead, and the crossing is protected by a stout wooden frame, so that a soldier with a gun on his shoulder will not be in danger of breaking the wire, **Figure 2**.

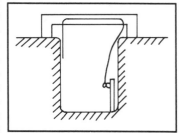

Fig. 2

15. Question. Is it possible to obtain good results from a collecting wire or loop buried in the ground, instead of being supported on stakes?

Answer. It makes no difference as far as efficiency of signal reception is concerned whether wire is buried in ground or supported on stakes, provided the wire is properly insulated. The method of burying the wire in the ground, is, however, open to many objections, the chief of which being that if anything does happen to the wire or its insulation, such as damage due to a shell, or an unlucky blow of a soldier's pick, etc., it is difficult to locate the injury. In actual practice, it often happens that for short distances the wire is buried in the ground. Furthermore, a loop of wire fastened to stakes is more easily moved than if the wire were buried, and this is quite often an important consideration, especially in sectors where activity prevails.

16. In the case where the antenna is a long insulated wire with its terminals connected to earth, the same care must be exercised to insure good insulation, as was described above in the case of the loop. The same method of supporting the wire by wooden stakes and insulators is made use of. The wire should be laid parallel to and as near as possible to the enemy's lines. Accordingly, it is usually placed in the first French trench. The positions of the earth connections in general are not important. The resistance of the earth connections should be as low as possible; the lower is the resistance the stronger are the signals. The French use as an earth connection a wire mesh buried in the ground with crystals of ammonium chloride.

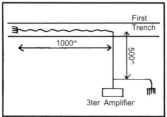

Fig. 3

17. A few figures will illustrate the importance of good earth connections. The diagram, **Figure 3**, shows a listening station consisting of a long wire, amplifier, and two ground connections. The impedance of the amplifier is 600 W, the impedance of the wire and earth is negligible. If the earth connections are each a single mesh one foot square, **Figure 4 (a)**, we have an impedance of 400 ohms at the earth connections, which is large compared to the impedance of amplifier. If each ground is made with two squares of mesh joined together, the impedance of the ground connection is 200 ohms, **Figure 4 (b)**. If one end of this last arrangement is buried with NH_4Cl, the impedence drops to perhaps 100 ohms, **Figure 4 (c)**; and if both ends are buried in NH_4Cl, the impedance drops to 40 ohms. This then, is a value small compared to the impedance of the amplifier, and there is then a chance of getting loud signals. It should be noted that the above values of the impedance of the earth connections are merely average estimates. In actual cases the values vary widely depending upon such factors as the nature of the terrain, the water content, etc.

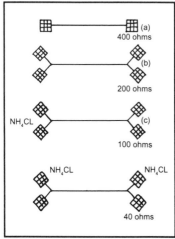

Fig. 4

18. The two leads to the loop, or the one lead of the earthed wire and another earthed lead, are brought into the dugout and attached to the T.P.S. (Low Frequency) terminals of a 3-ter amplifier. The electrical connections are shown in **Figure 5.**
It is of no importance whether the leads into the amplifier are twisted together or not, provided the insulation is good. The amplifier, in the dugout, rests on a table insulated from the ground by pieces of glass; the chair on which the observer sits is also insulated from the ground. The head phones and lead wires connecting the headphones to the 3-ter amplifier must be dry. If a person touches these leads with moist hands, a loud sizzling is heard and nothing more can be done until the leads are dried. Therefore, it is the practice to have three sets of head phones, one in use and two drying by the fire.

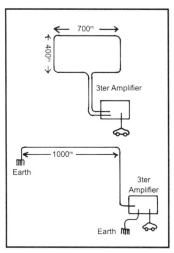

Fig. 5

Two or three extra amplifiers and a number of extra bulbs are kept at the station. Batteries are charged at the base post and are brought up when necessary.

19. Question. Is the 3-ter amplifier the only amplifier used in the listening station by the French at the present time?
Answer. Yes.

20. Question. Would higher amplification be advantageous?
Answer. Yes. The French authorities have recently recommended the trial of a four stage amplifier. There are two factors which limit the amount of amplification practicable, the first being noise from external sources which drowns out the signals, the second being noise produced in the amplifier itself. It is possible to eliminate in large part noise due to external sources, such as strays, etc., by the use of an insulated loop (as discussed later). Also, the 3-ter amplifier is not altogether free from internal noise. Therefore, it is believed that a four or five stage amplifier, provided it was noiseless, might be used to advantage.

21. Question. Is a dugout an entirely satisfactory place for a listening station?
Answer. A wooden house would be a much more suitable place for the listening station, because the difficulty of maintaining electrical apparatus in a high stage of insulation in the humid atmosphere of a dugout is considerable. But in view of the fact that the station must of necessity be situated in a position close to the enemy, and usually in a region of activity, the stations have perforce been established almost entirely in dugouts.

22. Question. Where is the best place to establish a listening station?
1st Answer. Obviously, it is advantageous to place the station at a point where the enemy's lines are close to yours, because if the enemy is near at hand, there is then a possibility of hearing what he is saying.
2nd Answer. A station, placed in a sector where occurs any activity such as

prevails before a battle, will certainly be able to hear messages of importance. For this activity means much telephoning and sending of messages to and fro from the first line trenches. At such a time various artillery units advance nearer to the first line trenches and use freely the T.P.S. buzzer sets, which, being powerful and connected to earth, are easy to hear.

23. Question. At what distance is it possible to get signals?
    Answer. T.P.S. buzzer sets, which are ground connected, give signals which may easily be heard at a distance of 3 km. Conversation over a single wire, ground connected, telephone system cannot be heard at a distance much exceeding 500 m. Communication over a two-wire system insulated from ground, is practically never intercepted.

24. Question. What arrangement of the enemy's wires offer the best possibilities for interception of signals by a listening station?
    Answer. In general, enemy communication lines parallel to the front offer the best opportunities for interception; whereas, lines perpendicular to the front are difficult to intercept. **Figure 6** shows a number of possible positions of the enemy's lines with respect to the loop of a listening station.

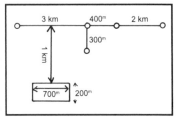

Fig. 6

25. Problem. Given a situation, as shown in **Figure 7**, where is a good place to lay the antenna for the listening station? It was useless to try a loop, or an earthed antenna, in back of the French trench, for the distance between the French trench and the enemy's trench was too great. It was also impracticable to lay any wires for any great distances in no man's land. The solution was finally effected as shown in the diagram. The antenna was laid in the river, insulated throughout its entire length. The antenna was thus fairly close to the enemy and in a position not likely to be discovered by the enemy's patrols. One end of the wire was earthed, and the other end was brought back to the station at the point where the French trenches were nearest to the enemy. (It was stated that the above problem was actually met and solved in the manner described.)

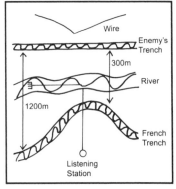

Fig. 7

26. Elimination of External Disturbances. The most serious difficulty which a listening station encounters is due to the presence of external electrical disturbances which produce sufficient noise to completely mask the signals which are desired to be read. The elimination of these undesirable disturbances is one of the most important problems which the listening station has to solve. The external disturbances are of two kinds, which we will call "strays" and "motor noises," respectively. Each kind will be considered in turn.

27. Elimination of "Strays." This class of electrical disturbances includes those due to natural causes, such as changes in potential of various portions of the ground or atmosphere within effective distance of the apparatus of the listening station. The effect is to cause a violent crackling and gurgling in the earphones. The "strays" are very erratic in intensity, but are liable to be strong at night time, in stormy weather, and in foggy weather. To suppress the

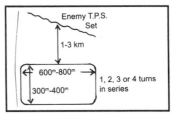

Fig. 8

strays, the loop antenna is employed. If a loop, well insulated from the ground, is used, and if all apparatus in the dugout is carefully insulated, the noises due to strays are in large part eliminated. The resistance between loop and ground should be 60,000 ohms or more. The earthed antenna under the same conditions, although giving louder signals for the same length of wire (as discussed in paragraph 31), is open to the objection that the strays are picked up in great abundance. The French officers emphasized very strongly their preference for the loop form of antenna. They considered it a much more useful arrangement than the ground connected antenna, and well worth the additional wire and extra care necessary for its construction and maintenance. **Figure 8** shows the usual size of loop and distance from enemy.

28. Elimination of "Motor Noises." By "motor noises" are meant noises arising in receiving circuit produced by induction from a motor or generator, either in a fixed position, or on trucks which pass by along a fixed route. We consider two cases.

29. (1) Source of noise in a different direction from source of signals.
This case may be represented by a motor nearby in a fixed position in friendly territory, or by trucks passing by on a road in friendly territory, **Figure 9**. To eliminate the motor noise, an earthed antenna is used with an additional extension, (a, b, Figure 9) on the side nearest the source of disturbance. The effects in the two branches a b and b c are equal and opposite, and hence cancel each other. This may be termed the method of opposition. It should be noticed that it is not possible to use an insulated loop in this case.

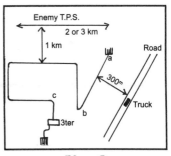

Fig. 9

30. (2) Source of disturbance in same direction as source of signals.
This case may be represented by a source of disturbance, such as a truck, at a considerable distance in back of the enemy's lines, as shown in **Figure 10**. In this case, the insulated loop antenna is employed. The truck is a distance away from loop which is great in comparison with width of loop. Therefore, the front and back sides of loop receive approximately equal and opposite effects, and hence the effects cancel. The signals received from the enemy's T.P.S. set, however, are strong, for this is at a much smaller distance away, and hence the effect in the near side of the loop is much stronger than in the far side of loop. If we connect loop to ground at A and B, and thus change to the ground connection

system, we get the T.P.S. signals increased perhaps twice, but the motor noises perhaps six times.

31. Comparison between insulated Loop and Earthed Antenna. The insulated loop antenna was found to give signals more distinct and more free from extraneous disturbances than the earthed antenna. The signals obtained by the loop are, however, weaker than those obtained by the earthed wire, the same length of wire being used in each case. An idea of the relative intensities obtained in the use of two forms of antenna is afforded by **Figure 11** and **Figure 12**. In each case, the signals obtained from the loop are of approximately the same intensity as those obtained from the earthed wire.

It is thus seen that a loop requires three or four times the length of wire to give as intense signals as a ground-connected antenna. The loop also requires greater care with respect to its insulation from the ground than is necessary in the case of the ground-connected wire. On the other hand, the loop antenna gives signals much more distinct and much less liable to external disturbances than the grounded antenna. In the opinion of the French officers, the advantages obtained by using the loop far outweighed the disadvantages. They spoke very strongly of their preference in favor of the insulated loop form of antenna.

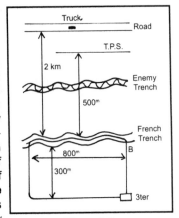

Fig. 10

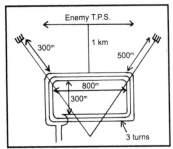

Fig. 11

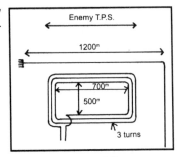

Fig. 12

Appendix F

Ground Telegraphy or T.P.S.

Land Division, O. C. S. O.
3-1-18. Confidential.

S. C. R. Pamphlet No. 10.

Description and Use of the SCR-71 Transmitter and the SCR-72 Amplifier in Forward Position Communication Work

Ground telegraphy is a means of communication which requires no wire connection between the sending and receiving station, but is different from radio telegraphy in that it involves the use of currents of comparatively low frequency such as can be detected directly by the telephone receiver, instead of currents of several hundred thousand cycles per second frequency, as in radio. This means of communication is carried out through the conduction of current by the earth, and the interception of some of the radiating lines of this current by suitable receiving instruments. The alternating currents which flow in the sending base (between the two grounded terminals of the sending instrument) spread out from the ground plates both vertically and horizontally and produce currents of similar frequency in the receiving base circuit by conduction and by electromagnetic induction. Geological conditions have a great influence upon the transmitting range. Very damp soil has been found to be unsuitable for this means of communication on account of its good conductivity, which results in the return lines of current flow not spreading out, as should be the case for good transmission.

SCR-71 T.P.S. Transmitter

The ground telegraph apparatus as used by the Signal Corps, U.S. Army, consists of a power buzzer for transmitting and a two-stage vacuum tube amplifier for receiving. The power buzzer SCR-71 is a sending device and in principle of operation it is the same as the ordinary Signal Corps buzzer but much more powerful and different in details of construction. It is usually referred to as the T.P.S. transmitter (from the French, "*Télégraphie par Sol*") and it consists of a high frequency buzzer which interrupts the circuit from a 10-volt storage battery through a small transformer. A condenser of 6 mfd. capacity is connected across the spark gap to suppress the sparking at the contact points. A telegraph key is also inserted in the circuit from the storage battery through the primary of the transformer and the vibrator. The secondary of the transformer is connected to the ground through the base wires and ground rods at two points not less than 50 yds. apart. By this means an alternating current of a frequency variable between 650 and 1700 cycles per second, and of about .4-amp. strength when the base resistance is not over 50 ohms, is caused to flow into the earth. These various frequencies are obtained by means of a set of weights which can be fastened singly or in pairs at the end of the buzzer armature, the following combinations being possible:

Fig. 1

SCR-71 T.P.S. POWER BUZZER

Large weight all the way out	650 cycles per second
Large weight, all the way in	750 cycles per second
Two small weights, all the way out	800 cycles per second
One small weight, all the way out	1000 cycles per second
One small weight, all the way in	1250 cycles per second
No weight	1700 cycles per second

The magnetic circuit of the transformer is completely metallic except for an opening at the top which is filled in except for the air gaps by a "V"-shaped iron piece attached to the under side of the buzzer armature. The best operation of the buzzer is obtained when the armature position is so adjusted that the air gap on either side of the projecting "V" iron is uniform. Adjustment to this position is made by loosening the nut and bolt through the yoke of the vibrator, when the armature pieces can be shifted slightly to bring them to the proper position. It is very essential that the buzzer contacts be kept clean and free of pits in order that a good tone may be secured. A small file is provided in the set for this purpose. A clear tone for each setting should be obtained by adjusting the thumb screw above the armature.

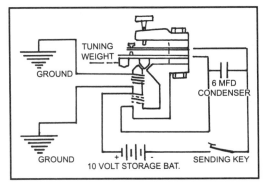

Fig. 2

POWER BUZZER WIRING DIAGRAM

The ground buzzer set has a range of from 2,000 yds. to 3,000 yds. under ordinary conditions, and messages have been received as far as 4,000 yds. under particularly favorable circumstances. It is not safe, however, to count on a range of greater than 3,000 yds. The power buzzer SCR-71 weighs about 9 lbs. and the 10-volt storage battery used to operate it weighs about 32 lbs. Four lengths of flexible insulated wire, 150 ft. long and carried on reels, are supplied with the buzzer for making proper connections to the ground rods. Twelve ground rods, two hammers and canvas carrying cases are provided with the set.

SCR-72 Low and High Frequency Amplifier

The SCR-72 amplifier is a two-stage vacuum tube unit which can be used either for receiving ground telegraph or radio by proper connection to the input terminals. The input impedance of the amplifier when used for radio telegraphy is about 20,000 ohms, and when used for ground telegraphy it is about 200 ohms. The amplification of energy received is about 10,000 times, and this is as great as can be used effectively under ordinary conditions of interference in either ground or radio telegraphy. In order to provide for a variation in the amount of amplification secured, telephone jacks are provided on the input side, at the end of the first stage and out the end of the second stage, so that three values of amplification can be obtained.

The filaments of the two type VT-1 vacuum tubes are supplied with energy from a 4-volt 100-amp-hr. storage battery. The characteristic of these tubes is such that there is little variation in their sensitiveness when the battery is fully charged and when it is nearly discharged. For this reason, no filament rheostat is required. A l.3-ohm resistance is connected permanently in the positive side of the filament circuit. This is not required for the tubes of some manufacturers, and in these tubes the positive terminal of the filament

Fig. 3

SCR-72 RADIO AND T.P.S. AMPLIFIER

is permanently connected to the brass base. A connection is installed in the amplifier from the socket to the positive side of the l.3-ohm resistance. The resistance is thus

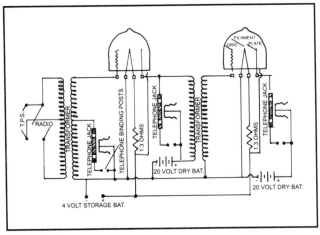

Fig. 4

WIRING DIAGRAM OF SCR-72 THREE-STAGE AMPLIFIER

automatically short circuited when a tube is inserted which has a connection between the positive filament terminal and the shell, or, in other words, when the positive side of the filament is grounded. The plate current is supplied by a 20-volt dry battery, and adjustment of the plate voltage is unnecessary.

The vacuum tubes employed should be handled with care, and no other batteries than those furnished for the sets should be used to supply the plate or filament currents. It is interesting to note that no adjustments are required in making use of this amplifier for either ground or radio work.

The vacuum tube amplifier is used for receiving only, consequently if two-way communication is desired, a buzzer and amplifier must be supplied at each end of the circuit. The SCR-72 amplifier is of American design and manufacture and weights with the case and accessories, about 27 lbs. These accessories include the telephone receivers, extra vacuum tubes, and an extra dry battery. In addition to these auxiliaries, the complete set includes a 4-volt, 100-amp-hr. storage battery weighing about 25 lbs., 600 ft. of antenna cord carried on reels in lengths of 150 ft. each, 12 ground rods and two hammers with the necessary canvas carrying cases.

Opening a Ground Telegraph Station

In using ground telegraph sending and receiving sets, special attention should be directed to the position of the ground rods of the sending and receiving stations relative to each other. The power buzzer is connected to the two sets of ground rods placed not less than 50 yds. apart. A straight line joining these earth connections is called the "sending base line." The receiving instrument or amplifier is similarly connected to ground rods, and the line connecting them is called the "receiving base line." These two base lines must be laid out in such a manner that a straight line joining the centers of the bases will make equal angles with each of them, the angles considered being on the same side of that line. The best position is that whereby the bases are exactly parallel and opposite to each other. This condition is shown in Fig. 5.

When two power buzzers communicate with the same receiving station from different directions, it is desirable that separate bases for the reception of signals from

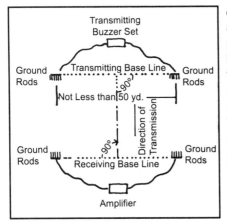

Fig. 5
BEST RELATIVE ARRANGEMENT OF
T.P.S. STATIONS

each sending station should be provided, as shown in Fig. 6. If it is impossible to provide two bases, the single receiving base should be aligned with respect to the two sending stations, as shown in Fig. 7, so that a straight line joining the centers of the bases will make equal angles with the two bases joined. This follows the general law first stated, as it is applied to each combination of receiving and sending stations. The correct relative positions of receiving and sending base lines may be established by the use of a compass which should always be utilized to insure this. Usually the angle between the base line and the line connecting the centers of the receiving and sending bases must be greater than 60 deg. to enable communication. Special at-

cation. Special attention should be paid to securing a good earth connection at the ends of both the sending and receiving base lines. Due to the nature of this system of communication, it is very easy for the enemy to pick up messages sent, and all communications should therefore be in code.

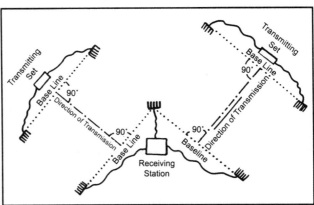

Fig. 6
PROPER ARRANGEMENT OF BASE LINES WHEN
ONE STATION IS RECEIVING FROM TWO OTHERS

In place of the ground rods furnished with the set, or in addition to them, various metallic bodies, like cartridge cases, etc., may be buried in the ground and connected to the wire. This provides a lower ground resistance and increases the range of the signals. In cases of very weak signals at the receiving station, or if very great range is desired, the sending buzzer may be operated on 20 volts without injury to the apparatus.

In some special cases, particularly for long distance signalling (1¹⁄₂ miles to 3 miles), the buzzer may be replaced by an alternating current generator of a frequency of at least 500 cycles (the generator used for the U.S. Signal Corps pack set, for

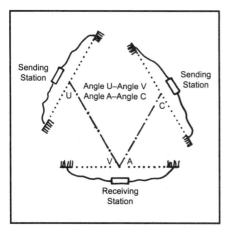

Fig. 7
ARRANGEMENT OF BASE LINES WHEN
ONE STATION IS RECEIVING FROM TWO
OTHERS AND IT IS IMPOSSIBLE TO LAY
OUT SEPARATE RECEIVING BASES.

instance). Communication in this case is very good and easily recognizable, due to the steady, musical note of the signals. This scheme is quite frequently used in the French Army, but no American equivalent has as yet been adopted.

The wires used to connect the T.P.S. apparatus (sending or receiving) to the two ground plates should always have a perfectly good insulation. They may then be laid on the ground, or even be buried, which is quite frequent practice at the sending stations which are generally in or near the first line of trenches. In no case should bare wire or lead-covered cable be used for making up the sending station, as signals could not be sent out to any distance. The weakness of the bare wire is obvious. With lead-covered cable, the metal sheath will short circuit the current leaving the ground plates of the sending station, instead of letting it spread out through the ground to the receiving station. At the receiving station the wires are seldom buried underground, as there is less danger of having them cut by shell fire, the receiving station being generally at some distance from the front line. It should be noted that lead-covered wire is not objectionable at the receiving station. However, when a station is used for two-way communication, ordinary insulated wire should be used. Other wire than that supplied with the equipment should be used only in case of emergency.

Use of the SCR-72 Amplifier in the Listening-In Service

The listening-in service consists in the picking up of enemy earth induction and telephone messages. Many schemes are used for this purpose, one of which is described below. Two grounds BB, Fig. 10, similar to those used for T.P.S. transmission, are installed at night as near as possible to the enemy trench and connected to the amplifier A by means of insulated, twisted pair flexible cord. Connection may also be made to the enemy barbed wire entanglement system. The amplifier A is set up in a deep and dry dugout. In case of a leaky telephone line in the enemy trench, the conversation will readily be heard at A, due to induction and conduction of the telephone currents.

One objection to this scheme is that, while interference traveling at right angles to the line BA is eliminated by the use of twister pair cord, interference traveling parallel to it is still free to act on the amplifier. Such interference is mainly due to our own T.P.S. sending sets working at close range and in the same trench.

To counteract such interference, two sets of ground plates, BB, CC, are used simultaneously as shown in Fig. 11. Each group of ground plates is connected by means of twisted pair cord to one of the coils b and c of a differential transformer, the two lines being run very close together. These two coils are wound in opposite directions, with the same number of turns. A third coil M, wound on the same core, is connected to the amplifier. If now a stray current should act on the system, it would affect both sets B and C equally, and the magnetic fluxes set up in the coils b and c, being equal and opposite, will produce no sound in the amplifier. If, however, an enemy conversation is taking place at X, the effect will not be the same in the two sets of ground plates, and therefore the fluxes set up in the coils b and c will be out of balance, whereby the signals and talking will be heard in the amplifier.

Possible Schemes of Eliminating Ordinary Interference

Two common forms of interference at the receiving station are those due to a. c. power lines running in proximity to the ground station, and those due to various other sending stations operating simultaneously. The interference due to power lines may be quite successfully cut out by connecting in series with the amplifier a resonating circuit tuned to the frequency of the interfering power line (see Fig. 8). By this means, practically all the energy of the interfering current is taken up in the resonating circuit in making it oscillate, allowing the signal current induced in the circuit to flow through the amplifier with less interference. With interference from other radio or T.P.S. sets, the connection of Fig. 9 may be used to advantage, the circuit LC being tuned to the frequency of the signals to be received and connected in parallel with the amplifier. Since the circuit is tuned to the incoming signals, the current of the corresponding frequency caused to flow in the amplifier is stronger than that due to the interfering signals, making it readily possible to distinguish the proper signals from the several heard.

There is no intention at the present time of supplying the necessary apparatus to carry out any of the above suggestions for dealing with interference. The ideas and drawings are presented simply as a matter of information.

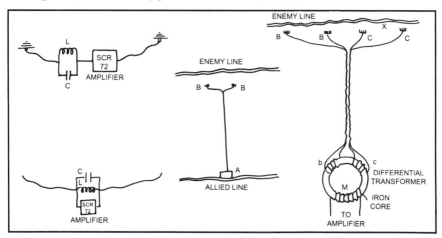

Fig. 8 CONNECTION OF SCR-72 TO MINIMIZE INTERFERENCE FROM POWER LINES – **Fig. 9** CONNECTION OF SCR-72 TO MINIMIZE INTERFERENCE FROM OTHER SENDING STATIONS – **Fig. 10** ARRANGEMENT OF SCR-72 FOR LISTENING-IN SERVICE – **Fig. 11** CONNECTION OF SCR-72 TO COUNTERACT INTERFERENCE IN LISTENING-IN SERVICE.

Appendix G

Shoulder Patch of the Radio Listening Service of the Signal Corps

In the 1960's, while on active duty at Fort Lee, Virginia, I donated my father's tunic and a photocopy of my father's original manuscript to the Army Quartermaster Museum at Fort Lee, Virginia. I distinctly remember that the First Army shoulder patch on the tunic had two small diamonds, overlapped, in the space under the bar of the A. Starting to work in 1992 with preparation for publication, I wrote to the museum and requested an opportunity to return and photograph the patch. I received a prompt answer that the uniform had been transferred to the Fort Dix Museum in 1984. When I contacted the Signal Corps Museum in Fort Gordon, Georgia, they had no record of a special shoulder patch for the Radio Listening Service. In May, 1994, I was informed that 2,000 artifacts had indeed been transferred from the Quartermaster Museum to the Fort Dix Museum. Fort Dix had eight tunics remaining and none were the proper one. In December, 1994, a letter to the Army Institute of Heraldry at Fort Belvoir provided a partial solution to this problem. They sent me a copy of memorandum No. 46 from Headquarters First Army, American Expeditionary Forces, France, dated 18 December 1918, which delineates patches for *officers* not assigned or attached to organizations or services. There were different designs under the bar of the A in every case, and the Signal Corps had an orange diamond located there. I do have one photo of my father which shows a very dark diamond under the bar and I very definitely remember that it was black and staggered over a white or very pale grey one of similar size.

In May, 1995, after again unsuccessfully searching for the patch at the Army Military History Institute at Carlisle Barracks, I was referred by Randy Hackenburg to Colonel David Kyle of Mason Neck, Virginia, who confirmed the findings of the Army Institute of Heraldry.

The tunic that I donated to the Quartermaster Museum at Fort Lee was a custom made one and had a cloth label on the inside pocket that said "The Hub, Baltimore". First Army orders Nos. 45 and 46 from mid-December, 1918 were probably the result of a widespread lack of uniformity in the design of shoulder patches. I firmly believe that the patch of the Radio Intelligence section of the Signal Corps was as I have

136

sketched in Figure 1 on this page. Order No. 45 officially eliminated it. My father changed the patch on the tunic the Army had issued to him but not on the one that he had paid for with his own money. One tunic for inspecting officers and MP's to see, another to wear on your own time. I know from personal experience how the attitude of soldiers can change when a war is over and you want to go home. Somehow, this patch has been removed from the Army Museum system.

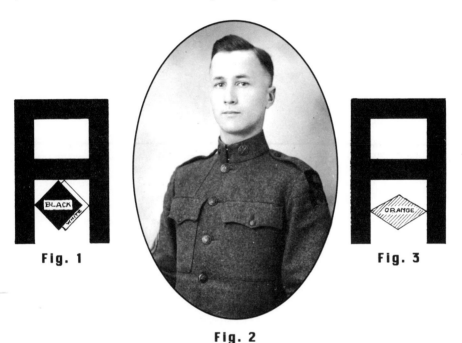

Fig. 1   **Fig. 2**   **Fig. 3**

Figure 1 is my memory of the patch. *Figure 2* is the only photo I have of my father that shows the patch and *Figure 3* shows the design forwarded to me by the Institute of Heraldry. I enjoy fantasizing that the diamond (in reality a square turned on its side) symbolizes clandestine listening, night and day.

ENDNOTES

CHAPTER 1

1. See Frederick C. Lubke, *Bonds of Loyalty, German Americans and World War I* (DeKalb, Illinois: Northern Illinois University Press, 1974).

2. Camp Meade was newly constructed in the summer of 1917 on land purchased from the Washington, Baltimore, and Annapolis Railroad. For a thorough understanding of how Fort Meade came to be in its present location see John E. Merriken, *Every Hour on the Hour, A Chronicle of the Washington, Baltimore & Annapolis Electric Railroad* (Dallas, Texas: Leroy O. King, Jr. 1993) pp. 43–49. For a good description of conditions in the fall of 1917 and the formation of the 313th Infantry see Jeffery Harlowe, *Your Brother Will, The Great War Letters and Diary of William Schellberg* (Ellicott City, Maryland: Patapsco Falls Press, 1992) pp. 13–17.

3. As early as November 18, 1918 a brief history of the Army Signal School at Langres had been created. This history lists the Radio Operators School as being operated separately from the school for mobile units. Some of the tactical work of the latter was replaced by listening-in station duty and the study of German. See *Notes on the Army Signal Schools, A.E.F.* (Army Signal Schools, A.E.F., November 18, 1918) p. 6. Record Group 120, Entry 403, A.E.F., National Archives, Washington, D.C.

4. As my father explains a little later in this chapter, P. T. B. is a term that came from the French. Some of the French soldiers said that it was "Post Telephone Boche"; others said "Post Telephone Battalion."

5. The individuals mentioned in this narrative were not transferred to the Signal Corps, Radio Intelligence Detachment, from the Army Signal School at Langres until 3 May 1918 per. par. 19, SO., 121 G. H. Q., A.E.F. 1918. See appendices A and B.

6. This was probably the C. Mark III amplifier. For photographs and technical description see "Issuances on various subjects relating to the Army Signal Schools." R. G. 120, Entry 405, N. A.

7. This refers to "Boite de Resonance" Nos. 2 and 3. R. G. 120, Entry 405, N. A.

8. It is interesting to note the following extract from Summary of Information for Divisional Headquarters dated March 7, 1918: "Cable Thrower" (From British Summary, March 4, 1918).

    > It would appear that the enemy use a cable thrower for forming an earth connection for listening set "loops."

One end of a steel wire is attached to the projectile, which serves as an earth pin. This pin is a hollow steel tube, weighted, and shod with a round nosed point. It weighs 14 pounds and is 3 feet 2 inches long.

The earth connection afforded by the pin being planted in the ground is supplemented by the contact formed between the steel wire and the barbed wire of the entanglement.

CHAPTER 2

1. See G. W. Haddow and Peter M. Grosz, *The German Giants, The German R-planes, 1914–1918* (London: Putnam, 1988) for a complete history of the development of the R-planes.

2. The records of the Signal Corps School at Langres shows that a one day course on gas warfare was given to as many soldiers as possible. I found no record of my father having taken it. This was probably a result of the fact that there was a great shortage of competent German-speaking radio operators. R. G. 120, E. 404.

3. See Albert Ettinger and A. Churchill Ettinger, *A Doughboy with the Fighting 69th* (Shippensburg, Pennsylvania: White Mane Publishing, 1992) for a photograph of this memorial service in progress, p. 113.

4. While the irritation of the French soldiers is understandable, it should be noted that the first active participation of American units had occurred on May 28, the date of the long German report from Nauen which is reproduced in the text. Troops of the First Division under Col. Hanson Ely had recaptured the Town of Cantigny. See Dumas Malone and Basil Rauch, *War and Troubled Peace 1917–1939* (New York: Appleton-Century Crofts, 1960) p. 39. See also John J. Pershing, *My Experiences in the World War* (New York: F. A. Stokes, 1931) vol. 2, p. 59.

5. My father translated this Treubel message as follows:

    "Hello! Hello! Katzenkus! It's Mueller—Call for Lieutenant Willman, is he there?"
    "Who is calling?"
    "Major Pfaltz wants to speak himself."
    "One moment."
    "Hello—Lieutenant Willman, at your order!"
    "How many gas shells do you still have?"
    "900 - 77's and not more than 80 - 150's".
    "I am sending you out of Kristkogal 3000 more 77's and not more than eighty 150's."
    "Now?"
    "Immediately."
    (click — click)
    "Hello! Hello! Herr Major Pfaltz!"
    "Malar talking."
    "Is he gone already? Damn it!"
    (click)

6. My father used the term Telefunken in writing this long note, which was added later. I believe this is the same as the Zimmerman Telegram incident. At the time this long note was added, Barbara Tuchman's *The Zimmerman Telegram* had not been popularized. Literal translation would be "radio wireless." Telefunken is also the name of a German commercial company. The only other incident involving telegraphy that I know of occurred in December, 1914 when the German foreign office sent a ciphered telegram to the German ambassador requesting help in blowing up Canadian Railways.

7. Velvet was the name of a brand of smoking tobacco.

CHAPTER 3

1. See Pershing, op. cit. vol. I, p. 25; Laurence Stallings, *The Doughboys, the Story of the AEF, 1917–1918* (New York: Harper & Row, 1963) pp. 162, 168; Albert Ettinger and A. Churchill Ettinger, *A Doughboy with the Fighting 69th* (Shippensburg, Pennsylvania: White Mane Publishing, 1992) pp. 135, 140–141.

CHAPTER 5

1. Pershing, op. cit., vol. II, pp. 175, 216–218.

2. The elimination of the St. Mihiel salient by the Americans had been originally suggested to Pershing by Foch in a memorandum in July 1918. Pershing's staff had suggested that the drive be carried at least as far as the railroad opposite the center of the position, perhaps even bearing eastward to assault Metz. Marshal Haig objected strenuously to this idea, since he felt that Allied attacks should be further in the north, in the area between the Belgian coast and the River Meuse. In fact the French and British would have preferred for American troops to be under the command of their generals. But Blackjack Pershing insisted that American troops would operate independently in France, preferably in an American Sector of the front. Pershing did agree, however, to halt the drive when the St. Mihiel salient was eliminated, and he kept his promise. See J. W. Stock, "Americans at St. Mihiel" in *Illustrated Encyclopedia of World War I* (New York, London, Toronto: Marshall Cavendish, 1986) pp. 2960–2968. See also Denis Winter, *Haig's Command, A Reassessment*, (London: Viking, The Penguin Group, 1991) p. 175.

3. For complete information on the goniometer see R. G. 120, E. 405 A.E.F., N. A., Washington, D.C.

CHAPTER 6

1. Pershing, op. cit., p. 341; Stallings, op. cit., pp. 216–217; Walker, Dale, "Frank Luke, WWI Balloon Buster," *Aviation Quarterly* (Air Trails: Plano, Texas, 1978) vol. 4, No. 4, pp. 370–381; Kenneth Munson, *Fighters, 1914–19* (New York: Macmillan, 1968) pp. 36, 114.

2. Domèvre en Haye, about eight kilometers southwest of Flirey. In the original manuscript my father spelt the name Domervre, but on military maps this is the only town that I have found that fits the location described. The spelling of names of both people and places is not always consistent in the text. Mistakes could either be made by my father himself or, more likely, by his secretary who was not the best typist and did not know foreign languages.

CHAPTER 7

1. Pershing, op. cit., vol. II, p. 270. See also Stallings, op. cit., pp. 218–219.

2. See Stallings, op. cit., p. 206. This kind of supply line jamming by Fieldgrade officers was not an uncommon occurrence.

3. Translation:
   "Good Morning"—"Now the war is over for you, isn't it?——
   "Max"—"Seat yourself this way. That's nice. You know we take care of ourselves. There is much to know. Where do you come from?"
   "From Baltimore"—"And you?"
   "Lieutenant Thirkel. My family is in Frankfurt. Do you know Germany?"
   "In 1908 I was there. I have relatives in Frankfurt. Perhaps the Fadé family is known to you."

"I don't know them. There are so many, there are so many."

4. Translation:

"Do you know how many Americans are already in France?"
"Oh yes, nearly two million."

5. My father thought that Thiacourt was twenty miles away. A check of the map shows that six would be a more likely figure.

PREFACE TO PART III

1. Stallings, op. cit., pp. 207–208.

CHAPTER 8

1. The 79th Division was a unit that was untried and only partially trained. Paschall states that the failure of this division to keep up with the rolling artillery barrage resulted in their being pinned down without artillery support, and they suffered high casualties. See Rod Paschall, *The Defeat of Imperial Germany* (Chapel Hill, North Carolina: Algonquin Books, 1989) pp. 186–187.

2. When I was trained as a medical soldier in 1944 and in a reserve hospital in the postwar period, medical evacuation had not changed substantially from what is here described for 1918. It took the introduction of helicopter evacuation and MASH Units in the Korean War to accomplish that quick trip to the operating table that saved so many lives. Undoubtedly American casualties would have been even higher in Vietnam without these advances.

3. Triage, or efficient use of medical and in particular surgical personnel to save the maximum number of lives, is another way in which combat surgery is markedly different than civilian surgery. The main mission of the Army Medical Department is to maintain fighting strength.

4. For a good description of the experiences of a 313th Infantry Regiment Doughboy who survived the battle for Melancourt see Jeffery Harlowe, op. cit., pp. 43–47.

5. The original manuscript at this point has the name Mitchelson typed in. This was crossed off by my father and Reilly was written in. Returning to study documents that I had previously donated to the Military History Institute at Carlisle Barracks, I discovered a letter written by Karl Singwald, dated April 19, 1933, from the Maryland War Records Commission that stated that a Captain James B. Everitt was in command of Company D of the 313th Infantry Regiment at Fort Meade and that Captain Charles Gilbert Reilly was in command at the opening of the Meuse-Argonne offensive. This is undoubtedly the reason my father changed the name of the company commander.

CHAPTER 9

1. For a photo of Cuisy on this same day see Pershing, op. cit., vol. II p. 322.

2. Hinrichs had previously been a diving competitor at Eagles Mere, Pennsylvania.

3. Pershing, op. cit., vol. II, p. 332.

4. Ibid., pp. 339, 352.

5. The Germans had followed what today would be called a "scorched earth" policy in evacuation. There were only two usable roads in the area. The destruction was more than vindictive. It had actual military value. See Philip Warner, "America's Offensive, The Argonne" in *Illustrated Encyclopedia of World War I* (New York, London, Toronto: Marshall Cavendish, 1986) p. 3044.

CHAPTER 10

1. For a more extensive description of the technical aspects and method of operation of this equipment see *Ground Telegraphy or T.P.S., Description and Use of the SCR 71-Transmitter and the SCR-72 Amplifier in Forward Position Communication Work* (Land Division, O. C. S. O., S. C. R. Pamphlet No. 10, 3-1 1918) and *"Notes on the Power Buzzer or T.P.S."* R. G. 120, E. 405, N. A., Washington, D.C.

2. See appendix F, Figure 4.

3. This conversational or musical note of machine gun fire has been noted by other authors. See Paul Fussell, *The Great War and Modern Memory* (New York: Oxford University Press, 1975), p. 202.

CHAPTER 11

1. See entry on Verdun, battles of, in *Encyclopaedia Brittanica,* vol. 23, Chicago, London, Toronto, 1955 Edition, pp. 75–79.

2. According to Paul Fussell this exploitation of moments of waxing or waning half light is one of the distinct hallmarks of Great War rhetoric. Op. cit., pp. 56–58.

CHAPTER 12

1. Translation: "With trade only will we come."

EPILOGUE

1. Luebke, op. cit., pp. 147–151.

SELECTED BIBLIOGRAPHY

Bach, Christian and Henry Hall. *The Fourth Division*. The Division, 1920.

Berry, Henry. *Make the Kaiser Dance: Living Memories of the Doughboy*. New York: Arbor House, 1978.

Czernin, Ferdinand. *Versailles, 1919, The Forces, Events and Personalities that Shaped the Treaty*. New York: Capricorn Books, 1964.

Ettinger, Albert and A. Churchill Ettinger. *A Doughboy with the Fighting 69th*. Shippensburg, Penna.: White Mane Publishing Co., 1992.

Fussell, Paul. *The Great War and Modern Memory*. New York: Oxford University Press, 1975.

Gilbert, Martin. *The First World War, A Complete History*. New York: Henry Holt & Co., 1994.

Higham, John. *Strangers in the Land, Patterns of American Nativism*. New Brunswick, N.J.: Rutgers University Press, 1955.

Luebke, Frederick C. *Bonds of Loyalty, German Americans and World War I*. DeKalb, Ill.: Northern Illinois University Press, 1974.

Malone, Dumas, and Basil Rauch, *War and Troubled Peace 1917–1939*. New York, Appleton-Century-Crofts, 1960.

Manchester, William. *American Caesar*. Boston: Little, Brown & Co., 1978.

Paschall, Rod. *The Defeat of Imperial Germany, 1917–1918*. Chapel Hill: Algonquin Books, 1989.

Pershing, John J. *My Experiences in the World War*. New York: Frederick A. Stokes Co., 1931.

Stallings, Laurence. *The Doughboys*. New York: Harper and Row, 1963.

Tuchman, Barbara. *The Guns of August*. New York: Macmillan, 1982.

Tuchman, Barbara. *The Zimmerman Telegram*. New York: Dell Publishing Co., 1965.

Winter, Denis. *Haig's Command, A Reassessment*. London: Viking, The Penguin Group, 1991.

Witcover, Jules. *Sabotage at Black Tom, Imperial Germany's Secret War in America, 1914–1917*. Chapel Hill, N.C. 1989.

An extremely valuable ten-volume general reference on World War I with various authoritative authors is the *Illustrated Encyclopedia of World War I* (New York, London, Toronto: Marshall Cavendish, 1986).

Also of interest is the fact that in the summer of 1995 I uncovered a hidden set of five volumes in my library that belonged to my father. The first volume, copyrighted 1915, has an introduction by President Taft and a flyleaf inscription in my father's handwriting: *Ernest Hinrichs, Christmas 1916*. This is yet another indication of how intense his interest in the war was even before he was drafted. Entitled *The Great War* (Philadelphia: George Barrie's Sons, 1915–1921), the primary author is George H. Allen, formerly of the University of Pennsylvania History Department and later of the Military Intelligence of the General Staff.

INDEX

GENERAL

PERSONS